Better Homes and Gardens®

Kids' Rooms
DECORATING
IDEAS & PROJECTS

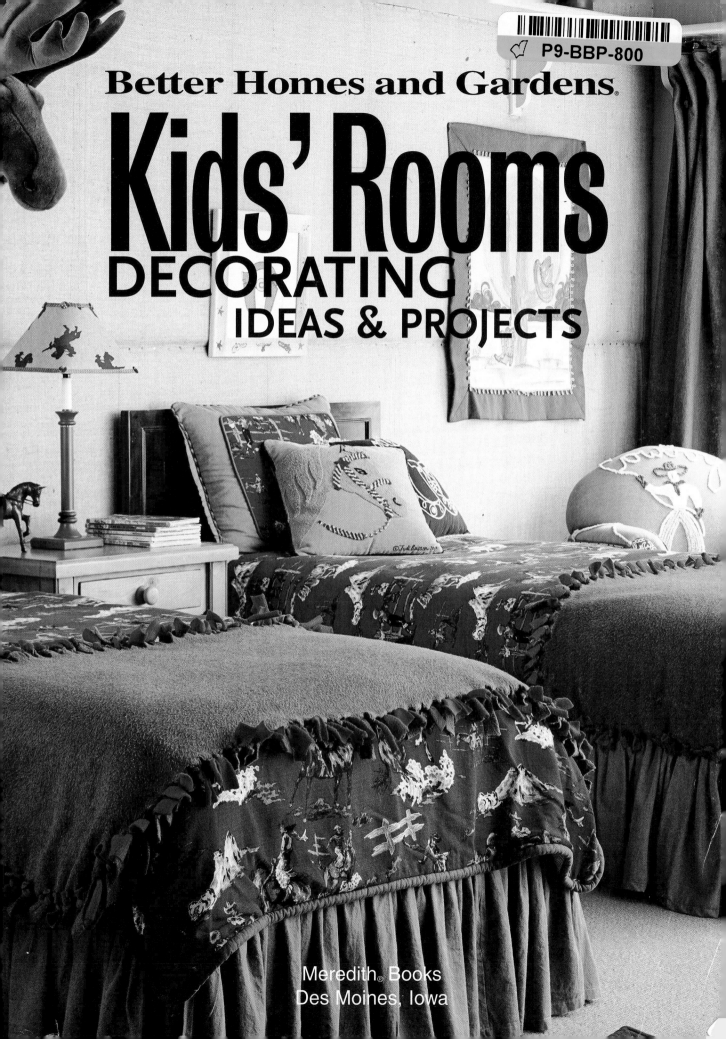

Meredith® Books
Des Moines, Iowa

Better Homes and Gardens® Kid's Rooms Decorating Ideas and Projects
Editor: Paula Marshall, Vicki Christian
Contributing Project Manager/Writer: Becky Mollenkamp
Contributing Graphic Designer: David Jordan
Copy Chief: Terri Fredrickson
Publishing Operations Manager: Karen Schirm
Senior Editor, Asset & Information Management: Phillip Morgan
Edit and Design Production Coordinator: Mary Lee Gavin
Editorial Assistant: Kaye Chabot
Book Production Managers: Pam Kvitne, Marjorie J. Schenkelberg,
   Rick von Holdt, Mark Weaver
Contributing Copy Editor: Susan Fagan
Contributing Proofreaders: Julie Cahalan, Sue Fetters, Heidi Johnson
Contributing Cover Photographer: Kim Cornelison
Contributing Indexer: Jana Finnegan

Meredith® Books
Executive Director, Editorial: Gregory H. Kayko
Executive Director, Design: Matt Strelecki
Managing Editor: Amy Tincher-Durik
Senior Editor/Group Manager: Vicki Leigh Ingham
Marketing Product Manager: Steve Rogers

Publisher and Editor in Chief: James D. Blume
Editorial Director: Linda Raglan Cunningham
Executive Director, Marketing: Steve Malone
Executive Director, New Business Development: Todd M. Davis
Executive Director, Sales: Ken Zagor
Director, Operations: George A. Susral
Director, Production: Douglas M. Johnston
Director, Marketing: Amy Nichols
Business Director: Jim Leonard

Vice President and General Manager: Douglas J. Guendel

Better Homes and Gardens® Magazine
Deputy Editor, Home Design: Oma Blaise Ford

Meredith Publishing Group
President: Jack Griffin
Executive Vice President: Bob Mate

Meredith Corporation
Chairman and Chief Executive Officer: William T. Kerr
President and Chief Operating Officer: Stephen M. Lacy

In Memoriam: E.T. Meredith III (1933–2003)

All of us at Meredith® Books are
dedicated to providing you with
information and ideas to enhance your
home. We welcome your comments and
suggestions. Write to us at: Meredith
Books, Home Decorating and Design
Editorial Department, 1716 Locust St.,
Des Moines, IA 50309-3023.

Contents

Rooms That Grow

With smart planning you can design a nursery with decor that easily will transition into your child's teen years.

Nurseries

Your newborn may never remember his or her nursery, but it is one decorating project you're unlikely to forget.

Toddler Girls

Whether your daughter is a little diva or sweet as sugar, you'll find a room here to suit her personal style.

Toddler Boys

Pack punch into your young boy's room by letting his hobbies serve as the inspiration for its design.

Teens

Join forces with your growing child to create a cool room that will please even the most finicky teen.

Other Spaces

Make children feel welcome in their bathroom or playroom by filling it with plenty of pint-size touches.

Getting Started

The abundant choices at children's decorating boutiques can be overwhelming. With so many furnishings, fabrics, and motifs, where do you start? This book will help you whittle the options to create a room that pleases you, your child, and your budget.

Before decorating a child's room, it pays to have a plan. Settle on a budget and stick to it. When deciding how much time and money to spend on the project, remember that a child can outgrow juvenile themes as quickly as he or she changes shoe sizes.

It's smart to think ahead. With every purchase and project for the room, consider how it will work as your child grows. The most efficient and cost-effective designs are those that are flexible and adapt easily to a growing child's changing needs.

Be creative and make certain your child's room looks great and functions well. Consider how the space will be used and accommodate those needs. Invest in high-quality pieces for the room's key elements (bed, dresser, and desk) because these items can survive into the teen years.

When it comes to colors and themes, choose what you love for the nursery. Then, as your child grows and develops strong opinions, involve him or her in decisions about colors and themes. A cooperative process helps ensure results everyone will love.

Get your child's input by flipping through this book to see what appeals to you both. The first chapter shows how one design can easily grow from nursery to teen retreat, while the next four chapters offer specific ideas for each stage of your child's life. Chapter 6 shares ideas for creating a kid-friendly bathroom or playroom. The last chapter, beginning on page 126, shows you how to re-create many of the creative projects featured in this book.

Spend some time taking in all the information this book has to offer and then head to that decorating store with confidence. After all, decorating a special bedroom for your child should be a fun and creative experience you'll never forget.

Rooms That Grow

Baby

With careful planning you can create a nursery that with just a few tweaks will remain appealing into your child's teen years. The keys are buying convertible items, choosing a timeless color palette, and spending just a weekend at each stage of your child's life to update the look.

Furniture is the most important (and expensive) element in a room that is expected to grow with the child. This inventive space uses a suite of alterable Swedish-inspired furnishings. Each of the major elements can change to perform new functions. The crib becomes a junior bed, the changing table converts into a desk, and the two shelving units join to create one larger armoire.

Nothing does more to change the look of the room as your child becomes a toddler and later a tween than a fresh coat of paint. Changing wall colors is an inexpensive and easy way to overhaul the

continued on page 12

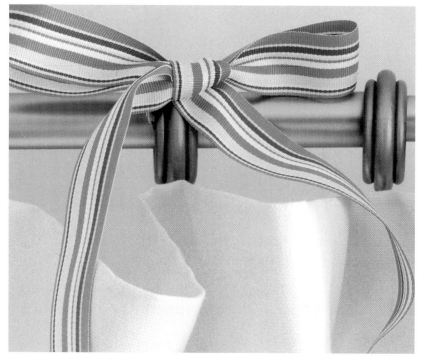

Left: Pretty ribbon tied around each curtain ring adds a tender little-girl touch. The ribbons are easy to remove later when she outgrows the "sugar and spice" look.

Above: A set of double shelves offers more than enough space to stash baby stuff. Store diapers and clothes behind closed doors on one side and put stuffed animals and photos on display on the other. Tuck sassy buckets below for child-level storage.

Opposite: Yellow walls with a low wainscot stripe of pink are a cheery backdrop for the soft and sweet accessories in this girl-friendly nursery.

Note: All photographs in this section are by Kim Cornelison.

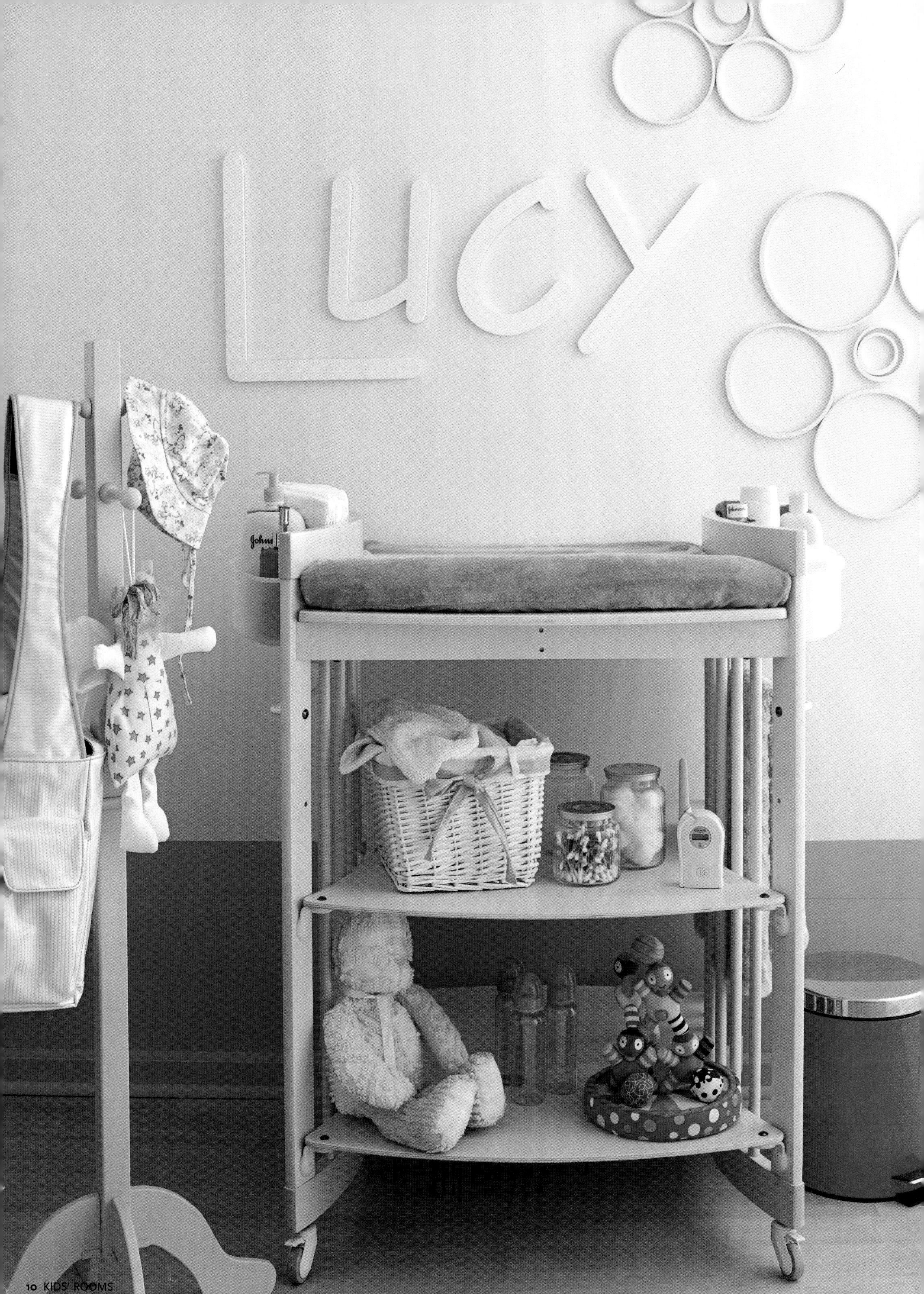
Lucy

Opposite: This simple-looking changing table is actually a complex piece of furniture. It can later be reconfigured to create a study space when your daughter enters school. In the meantime go overboard on cute with loads of pink accessories and her name on the wall.

Below: A painted stripe along the base of the walls introduces girlie pink. A simple panel of fabric sewn to the bottom of the curtains continues the stripe. The floral bedding hints at the more grown-up look to come.

Your daughter won't remember her nursery so make it a room that is special to you. Just remember to think ahead while planning the space. Smart choices now will reduce headaches and expenses later.

Toddler

space and make it clear that your child is growing up.

This room, designed for a daughter, starts as a sweet yellow nursery, changes into a fun green toddler room, and finishes as a bold orange tween suite. Choose colors that work well together; selecting the same intensity, or brightness, of each hue will help. A unified palette means that many accessories can remain as the room evolves. This streamlined approach saves money by reducing the number of things that must be repurchased and replaced.

With a color palette selected, focus next on choosing fabrics. Again, finding patterns that work well together is important. Lively stripes are easy to live with and age well. Pair them with polka dots and flowers for a more energetic look.

Simple window panels are easy to replace, while fabric shades are more complicated to make. This room kept

continued on page 16

Right: With the crib converted into a tot-size bed and a fresh coat of apple green paint on the walls, this colorful room suddenly feels more grown-up.

Opposite: A simple ribbon canopy adds a special touch to your growing girl's bed.

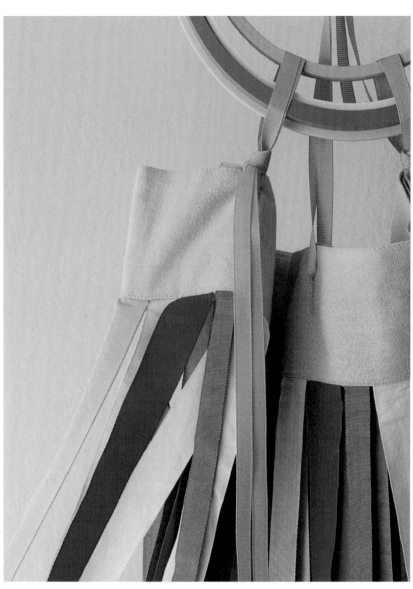

MOVING FORWARD

Though your kids' tastes will change as they grow from precious baby to opinionated teen, some bedroom staples remain the same. Make sure to invest most of your money in these three classics:

• Bed: Buy a crib that converts into a junior bed and then add a double bed later. Or buy a regular crib and then later add a larger bed that can go from toddler to adult.

• Desk: Choose a desk that can be raised and lowered. Give your toddler a pint-size chair and let her use the desk for art projects. Switch to a full-size chair and raise the desk when your child is ready to spread out textbooks instead of crayons.

• Shelves: From diapers to backpacks, your child will have lots of stuff to store and display. Pass up a cutesy, juvenile shelving unit and instead buy a simple one that will withstand the test of time.

Opposite: As your daughter begins to have more opinions about her room, let her make decisions about what to display on the shelving unit. She may want to add a stereo or more grown-up toys, but she probably won't be ready to give up all the trappings of youth, such as a stuffed animal collection.

Above: To update the look at the window, keep the same panels used in the nursery but add a slightly more sophisticated striped Roman shade. Another simple way to change the look is to update the finials.

Above right: Once your daughter is old enough for a regular bed, load it with pillows. Add to the cheery palette with a plethora of fun patterns and colors.

Right: Diapers are finally yesterday's news. Celebrate by converting the changing table into an arts-and-crafts station that allows her to express her budding inner artist.

Tween

the same panels for the first two stages and used the same shades for the last two. That simple choice equated to big money savings. Similarly, many of the pillows from the junior bed found their way onto the tween's full-size bed.

The final step is to add age-appropriate accessories that fit the room's look. In a nursery it's appropriate to choose soft and sweet items, such as stuffed animals, wicker baskets, and ribbon-trimmed accents. As your child ages, however, you'll want to inject a bit more attitude to reflect his/her growing sense of style. This toddler room has plenty of spunk but retains its innocence, while the tween space is more grown-up and a bit rebellious.

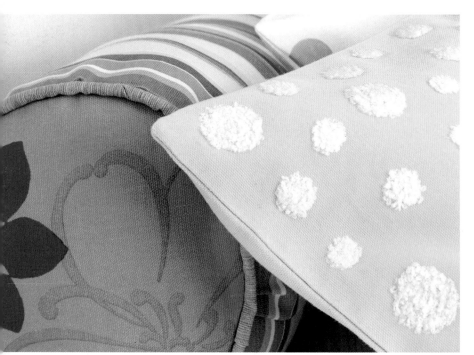

Above: As your daughter enters her tween years, she'll need her desk to function more like an office than an art studio. Turn it into Homework Central with the addition of a computer, message board, and shelves.

Left: With this final decor switch, keep some of the pillows from the junior bed but add a few new ones to coordinate with the updated window treatments and bedding.

Opposite: In the final phase of this evolving room, a full-size bed replaces a junior bed and the walls get a coat of bold orange paint. The trendy decor makes it clear this room's occupant is no baby.

Right: For a marked change in a tween's room, cover the walls with painted corkboard tiles. This is a fun addition that gives her plenty of space to hang notes, posters, and photos of friends. Paintable, adhesive-back circles add dimension and a burst of energetic color.

Below: Update the windows one last time by adding punchy floral panels that match the bedding. Keep the Roman shades to save money and effort.

Opposite: By her preteen years a girl is often becoming fashion conscious. Give her growing wardrobe a home by combining the two narrow bookshelves into one larger armoire with frosted doors.

At this age your daughter will have definite opinions about what she wants in her bedroom. Prepare to compromise on some of the things you want and to stand firm on the issues that are most important to you.

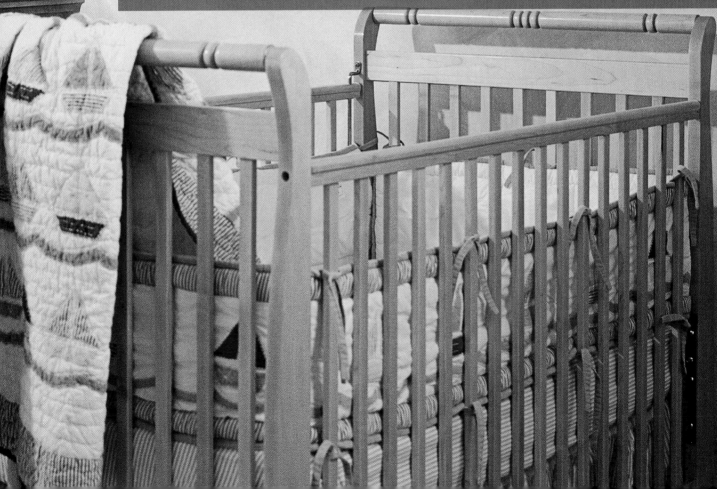

Nurseries

Quilted Inspiration

When faced with the daunting task of decorating a nursery, it can help to start with an inspiration piece. Find something you love—this is the item to splurge on—and then make it work for the room. In this space a fruit-theme quilt guided the decisions for everything else in the room.

The pricey quilt ate up much of the decorating budget, so the remainder of the room's costs had to be kept to a minimum.

A new crib joined a vintage rocker that was painted and re-covered to match the room. A decades-old armoire got a fresh coat of white paint and checkered knobs from a home center. White paint and baby-friendly fabric also transformed a tapestry-covered stool.

Save even more money by eschewing custom bedding. Select a collection of coordinating fabric—like the yellow and

green gingham, and a subtle blue-on-blue floral here—to make bumper pads and a small quilt for the crib. Skip pricey draperies and instead install sun-blocking roller shades. Hide them with a valance of paper lanterns, which can be found online for just a few dollars each.

Although blue is the traditional choice for boys' rooms, it easily works for girls too. Balance blue walls with a few ultrafeminine accents, such as pink accessories and a curvy chandelier. By stitching new and vintage together, you can create a nursery that's stylish but not costly.

Opposite: Bold blue walls and contrasting white furniture add style power to this tiny space. Although blue is often reserved for boys, delicate touches such as the embroidered linens and pastel accents make this room a feminine favorite.

Below: A quilt dotted with bananas, pears, and flowers served as inspiration for this nursery. To round out the stylish, budget-friendly nursery, Mom recycled furnishings, used high-impact paint, and showed some creativity with accessories.

Below right: In the crib store-bought pillows commingle with pillows crafted from antique linens. The pillows are moved to the floor while baby sleeps in the crib.

A room is more interesting when there is a story behind a few key pieces in it. Handmade touches make a space special.

Bright Side

Splashing a nursery with bold colors is a great way to create a room with staying power. A bright and cheery nursery is a particularly smart choice if the sex of your bundle of joy will be a surprise. Plus, without stereotypical pastels, a room will easily transition to an older child's room.

Rather than little-boy blue, happy turquoise coats these walls. Instead of little-girl pink, magenta is used sparingly but with impact. Bits of canary yellow and lime green round out the hot color scheme. White woodwork keeps the intense colors under control.

To further boost its staying power, the room is filled with valuable history lessons. Instead of letting family heirlooms waste away in boxes and drawers, this mom repurposed them in the nursery. An embellished tablecloth, passed down through three generations, is salvaged as a pretty crib skirt.

Vintage charm also can be functional, as witnessed by the painted furniture and suitcases used for storage. With its burst of juicy colors and comforting connections to the past, this nursery is a happy place to grow up.

Right: Remove the diaper-changing pad from a traditional changing table and what's left is a useless piece of furniture. Instead of baby-specific furniture, think long-term by adapting items you already own. A changing pad covered with stain-resistant fabric was added to this hand-me-down buffet; attach a guardrail for extra safety.

Opposite: This colorful nursery offers charm, function, and staying power. The saturated wall color, painted furniture, and simple linens can last from a child's infancy into the tricky tween years.

PAINT IT PRETTY

Holding on to an heirloom dresser or chair is pointless if it is left to languish in storage. Whether it is slightly banged up or simply doesn't match your decor, antique furniture can gain new life with a fresh coat of paint.

In this room one vintage dresser got a jolt of the new and now with bold magenta paint, while another received a lime green coat. The fun colors are in keeping with the style of this bright nursery, and the paint masks less-than-perfect wood finishes.

For a professional-quality finish sand the surface smooth with a fine-grit paper. Next apply a coat of water-based enamel primer; let dry. Apply several thin coats of semigloss latex paint. For extra protection and durability, add a top coat of water-based polyurethane.

FOR INSTRUCTIONS ON
MAKING FABRIC-COVERED
ART, SEE PAGE 128.

BARGAIN BIN
Decorating a nursery from scratch can cost a pretty penny. Save some cash—without scrimping on style—with these quick and easy ideas.
• Check out the calico section at the fabrics store. The fabrics come in myriad colors and patterns and cost just $1 to $2 a yard. Use the fabrics to make throw pillows, frames, and even crib bedding.
• To create simple sheer curtains, use the entire width of the fabric so you have to hem only the top and bottom edges. Quickly hang the curtain panels from a rod with ribbon loops, secured with a sew-through button.
• Search the house for everyday items to use as stamps, such as pencils, coins, or sponges.

Sea of Color

It's easy to go overboard when working with a theme, but this lively nursery incorporates several motifs that can be easily modified over time. Pastel paint and fabric projects create a spirited style that will transition to the toddler years and beyond.

The aquatic design starts with a pool of pastel hues on the walls. Mermaids and other oceanic images contribute major charm when used sparingly on the curtains, bumper pads, changing-table slipcover, and mobile.

Much of the design, however, comes from simple graphic shapes that will transition perfectly into the future. Dots, stripes, and scallops are found on the walls, pillows, storage bins, and other accessories. Together the motifs impart an ocean, but it is not over the top. By pulling out the water-theme patterns and inserting a new design—say, flowers—the room will quickly take on a new look without major redecorating.

Although the painted walls have a big impact, the creative details make this room special. Cube pillows are appliquéd with a different image on each side and embellished with ruffles and piping. Fabric-covered hatboxes, embellished with ribbon and trims, create pretty storage. Small glass knobs added to a display shelf are a good place for hanging baby clothes and accessories.

Opposite: The lighthearted mermaid fabric used on the bumper pads and curtains launched the room design. Numerous pastel paint hues plucked from the fabric play up the walls, mirror, and storage boxes and help stretch the decorating budget. Coordinating fabrics in stripes, checks, and dots add interesting dimension.

Left: Office storage goes to work housing baby essentials on the changing-table shelves. A tiered desk caddy is the perfect size for storing lotions, soaps, and other baby goods.

Below: To create a focal point in a room with little architectural character, angle a painted armoire in a corner and top it with hatboxes. A simple painted design of waves and dots forms a lively backdrop that accentuates the striped and mermaid fabrics.

FOR INSTRUCTIONS ON THIS PAINTED WALL TECHNIQUE AND FOR MAKING AFFORDABLE FRAMED ART AND HATBOX STORAGE, SEE PAGES 128-129.

Bold Move

Every mom-to-be wants the nursery to stimulate her baby's senses and warm her baby's heart. Accomplish this mission with a color-block wall of lively hues and a room filled with sentimental furnishings and accessories.

Start the look with a graphic grid wall in an invigorating palette—from hot pink and orange to blue and sunny yellow. Play with paint chips at a home center until you find the right combination. Use layers of fun fabrics—polka dots,

checks, stripes—as bedding and window treatments and to cover furnishings and other accessories.

Give hand-me down furniture or relics from your childhood an updated look with a fresh coat of paint. This old crib looks modern with new industrial-size casters and a wispy bed skirt made from sheer window treatment fabric. A long-forgotten rocking chair is refreshed with new ruffle-edge cushions topped with a colorful pillow.

Storage in this nursery is mostly hidden. Drawers and shelves keep clutter at bay behind the closet doors, toy-stuffed baskets can tuck away under the crib, a child-size cabinet hides dolls and stuffed animals, and pockets allow the slipcovered ottoman to pull double duty as storage.

Forget quaint pastels and the matching crib and changing table. Blend bold color with old furnishings to create an energetic nursery that melds past and present.

FABRIC MAKEOVERS

FABRIC MAKEOVERS

One of the simplest ways to add softness and interest to a room is to fill it with interesting fabrics. Here are a few ideas for using fabrics from this colorful nursery:

• Reduce the black-hole effect below a crib with a bed skirt. An airy sheer makes this small room feel larger. This skirt gains its fluffiness from a gathering stitch along the top; it is grounded by a band of ticking fabric along the bottom.

• Add pockets to a slipcovered ottoman for extra storage space. To make, cut fabric (use leftover scraps or even a pocket from a worn pair of jeans) to the desired size, fold the bottom and side edges under slightly, and iron. Fold the top over a piece of elastic; sew closed over the elastic. Pin each pocket to the slipcover, then stitch in place.

• Give a musty, old rocking chair new life with a simple no-sew technique. Strip the old cushions, glue on new foam, and then staple fabric over the foam. To hide the staples attach a ruffle or other trim around the edge with hot glue.

Above left: A wall painted with bold color blocks is a stimulating canvas in this nursery. The energetic wall is tempered by softer elements, including a wispy sheer with a leaf design, ruffles, and bows.

Above right: Pull colors from the room when choosing bedding. These graphic bumper pads feature hand-appliquéd birds. For a no-sew option, embellish a ready-made bumper with iron-on fabric decals.

FOR INSTRUCTIONS ON MAKING HANGER HOOKS, SEE PAGE 129.

Tickled Pink

Let your girl be a girl in a nursery that's all about feminine frills. Mix soft pink fabrics with shabby-chic furnishings to create a nursery your daughter will love for years.

Start with a neutral background of white walls. Colorful walls demand that everything in the space coordinate with them, while a mixture of accessories in different shades will always work with white. For cottage-style charm fill the spare space with vintage furnishings.

Scour thrift shops for fabulous finds. You can transform a piece of furniture with a coat of paint, so look for classic lines instead of color. The trunk and shelves in this room went from drab brown to bright white. The pint-size table and chairs aren't a matched set, but once the chairs are painted hot pink and the table is treated to color-coordinated ball fringe, they look picture-perfect.

Accent a nursery with fabrics that have a timeless quality. As your child grows, classic choices can be used in other spaces. Here a pretty green and pink floral fabric accents pillows and the crib; the strong pattern enlivens the white-walled room. Throw pillows in complementary fabrics add texture.

Opposite: A wicker settee plumped with punchy pillows is the perfect place to snuggle up and read to your tot. This sweet suite is accented with pops of pretty pink, from tyke-size chairs and a ball-fringed table to floral pillows and gingham curtains.

Above right: A painted flea market shelf doubles as a decorative accent and functional storage. Various containers corral baby goods now, but with their classic good looks they can be used in another space later.

TIMELESS TIPS

Children can quickly outgrow their room's style. Here are tips on using items that transition easily to new styles or can be moved to another part of the house:

• Furniture: Nursery basics, such as the crib, always should be current and meet safety standards. But antiques such as the settee and side table in this room add character and are appropriate for any age.
• Pattern: Time-tested fabrics, such as plaids and florals, can transition from nursery to little girl's room and beyond. Use baby-oriented fabrics sparingly on a few changeable and inexpensive pieces, such as the crib bedding or throw pillows.
• Accessories: Plates, trays, and old paintings are inexpensive, colorful ways to decorate nursery walls. When the child is older, mix in some larger artwork and posters.

Tailored Toile

No rule says a nursery has to be cutesy. A sophisticated toile pattern and sparing use of color make this room sweet enough for baby but stylish enough for Mom and Dad.

An elegant blue-and-yellow toile provides allover pattern that demands to be noticed. A mix of gingham, patchwork, and soft chenille fabrics tempers the formality of the wall design. Windows are outfitted with white plantation shutters that adjust to control light at naptime.

The crisp look also matches a host of simple white furnishings. The white-painted pieces add kid-friendly contrast to the room's darker, traditional wood pieces, some of which are family heirlooms.

Spare no detail in accessorizing a nursery. The toile theme is carried right down to the blue-and-white teddy bear on the changing table. Duckling accents, including one on a chenille blanket draped over the crib, are a lighthearted contrast to the more formal hunting scene on the toile wallpaper and shams.

Thoughtful design ties together everything in this nursery to create a warm room that will grow with the child or easily convert to a cozy guest room.

Opposite: The hunting-theme toile wallpaper sets a sophisticated tone for this little-boy-blue nursery. Healthy doses of white and pale yellow prevent the busy pattern from becoming overwhelming.

Right: A distressed dresser makes a cozy changing table and can be embellished or painted as the child grows up. Guardian angels on an antique architectural fragment hanging above the dresser watch over baby. The toile teddy bear is a finishing touch.

Right: Wide white frames around black-and-white photos of little toes and feet provide visual relief from patterned wallpaper. Stacked wicker baskets lined with gingham fabric are stylish, functional, and space-saving catchalls for toys and clothing.

Make family antiques more livable by mixing them with new items.

A simple room filled with classic accessories creates comfortable style.

Boyish Charm

A primary color scheme doesn't have to be loud and flashy. This red, yellow, and, blue nursery uses muted tones, pretty patterns, layers of fabric, and casual painted furnishings to create a comfortable cottage style that is sweet and charming, perfect for a little prince.

Although cottage design is popular in girls' rooms, the relaxed look can take on many forms. Add touches of blue, green, and cream to a multicolor cottage scheme to give it little-boy style. Balance feminine floral fabrics with more masculine designs.

A patchwork crib bumper is the perfect leaping-off point for the design. A mix

of faded versions of primary colors—all lifted from the bumper—gives the room colorful appeal. A custom-made crib skirt, window treatment, glider cushions, and closet panels made of vintage-style fabrics round out the room's fabrications.

Heirloom furnishings coupled with painted pieces take a leading role in the room and make it a snap to take the room to the next stage of your child's life. Fold in wire ledges, a sage rug, framed vintage prints, and blue-and-white pillows for boyish finishing touches.

Opposite: A fun mix of patterns—dots, plaids, and florals—creates visual interest in a nursery. The yellow walls and red fabrics are given a boyish touch with shots of blue in the crocheted blanket, glider, and pillows.

Left: Add a bright dose of color to the nursery with an inexpensive flea market chest coated in fire-engine red paint. Top the piece with boy-friendly accessories.

Above: A soft stuffed animal is a sweet accent to the blue-and-white pillows and accessories in a boy's nursery.

Sail Away

A nautical theme gives a boy's room a cohesive look and staying power. An anchors-aweigh wall treatment and seaworthy accessories can be altered or swapped out as the child grows, taking him from infancy into his teen years.

Start with a crisp color scheme of red, navy, and yellow; these strong colors provide plenty of visual stimulation for a developing mind. A backdrop of neutral white is a soothing relief from the more vibrant hues.

Take the theme wall to wall with a large-scale paint treatment. Cover the bottom two-thirds of the walls with swirls of blue. Apply several shades of blue glaze with a damp sponge, using a circular motion to create the illusion of waves. Top off the watery design with stenciled sailboats and roping. When the child is older, repaint the walls in subtle stripes or a bold plaid.

Limit furnishings to a few essentials and select finishes that blend with the rest of the room's palette. Avoid clutter by filling the room with only a few accessories. Down the road these small items can be exchanged for larger accessories, such as posters or nautical flags. Finish the nursery with a sailboat-motif crib ensemble that will allow your little sailor to drift off across a sea of dreams.

Opposite: Let the crib bedding you choose guide the nursery design. In this room the linens' regatta of sailboats inspired a nautical design that repeats on the walls, windows, furnishings, and accessories.

Below: Transform a corner shelf into a whimsical lighthouse that doubles as a stylish storage and display unit. Add a gabled roof using scrap wood. Cover the new design with red and white stripes and lightly sand the unit for an aged look.

FOR INSTRUCTIONS ON MAKING THIS NAUTICAL-THEME WINDOW TREATMENT AND TIEBACK, SEE PAGE 130.

Nervous about decorating an entire room on your own? A theme makes it easy. Stores often group items by theme, making it simple to pick out coordinated bedding and accessories.

Family Folklore

Put down roots in a bright and lively nursery that honors your family's heritage. Designing your baby's room with an eye on tradition is a great way to teach him or her about family history and continue family customs. This sweet nursery celebrates the parents' Norwegian and Irish backgrounds.

Begin with an inspirational piece and build the room's color scheme and design around this keepsake item. For inspiration research family photographs, books, prints, paintings, folklore sayings or poems, and dishware. In this nursery white chenille from the great-grandparents' wedding bedspread was turned into blocks for the quilt and used in the bumper and ties on the crib.

Scandinavian colors are rich and cheerful, which provided interesting design possibilities for this nursery. The hues are introduced through rosemaling, a Norwegian folk-painting technique. Although the design typically is painted on a dark surface with jewel-tone colors, this room gives it a modern twist with pastel paints on white furniture. Hire a trained rosemaling painter to design one-of-a-kind patterns, such as flowers, scrolls, and teardrops.

Right: The charming photos of Norwegian children above the crib once were part of a poster hanging in Mom's childhood bedroom. The images were hand-tinted and framed for a fresh but familiar look.

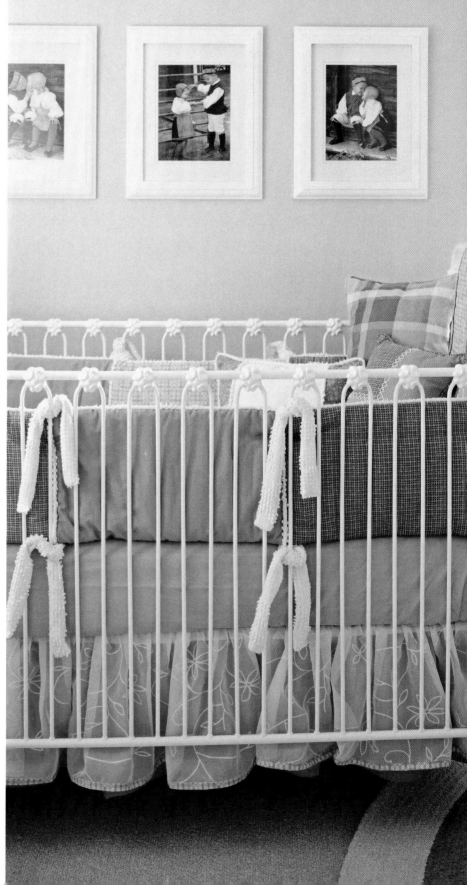

If you are leaving the sex of the baby a surprise for delivery, choose a variety of pastel colors that would suit a boy or a girl.

Above: The heirloom corner bookcase saves space in this 9×14-foot bedroom and provides ample room for a display of Nordic books.

FOR INSTRUCTIONS ON MAKING SHADOW-BOX ART, SEE PAGE 131.

Double Duty

Planning a nursery for more than one baby can multiply the fun as well as the challenge, especially when the room is for a boy and a girl. Make a bedroom twin ready with a little decorative and organizational ingenuity.

Start with a gender-neutral foundation of yellow-and-white striped walls, white woodwork, white furniture, and wood floors. Introduce a pink-and-blue color scheme through well-chosen details.

Distinguish each baby's area with different sheets—blue stars for him and pink pigs for her—and bumper pads. Tie the look together with a multicolor gingham fabric for the window treatments, crib dust ruffles, and changing-area details and accessories. Line simple window valances with pink or blue fabric and hang them from tension rods. Tack back a flap with a plain button hidden by a decorative bow.

For a changing table, top a dresser with a changing pad that can be removed when the twins move out of diapers. Touches of metallic silver on the mirror, picture frames, and shelves over the closet are like icing on the cake.

Above: Divide a gender-neutral background down the middle with splashes of blue on one side and pink on the other for a room suited for a twin brother and sister.

Opposite top: A little elbow grease and some paint can make any thrift store mirror match your decor. If the mirror is missing, a glass company can cut one to fit the frame.

Opposite bottom: If the nursery lacks dual closets, divide a single space for his-and-her storage. Remove doors for easy access.

FOR INSTRUCTIONS ON MAKING FABRIC-COVERED KNOBS, SEE PAGE 131.

FOR INSTRUCTIONS ON MAKING FABRIC-COVERED KNOBS, SEE PAGE 131.

DIVIDE AND CONQUER

Twins are twice the fun, but they don't necessarily need twice the stuff. Save money and space by investing in quality items that the little ones can share.

• Infants can share the nursery's biggest-ticket item: the crib. There are L-shape or curved corner cribs specifically designed for multiples, but these options are more expensive than traditional cribs and require special bedding. In a regular crib use a rolled-up towel or crib divider to keep the children separated once they learn to roll over. When sharing a crib begins to interrupt sleep, invest in a second crib or, if they are ready, move the children into toddler beds.

• You also can get away with buying just one dresser, changing table, playpen, bathtub, and swing.

41

On the Wall

A nursery requires lots of essentials—a crib, changing table, rocking chair, and more. With all of those furnishings, the room may lack floor space for additional storage. Create extra space for stuffed animals, clothes, and toiletries by stealing space on the walls.

Maximize a nursery's overlooked vertical space by hanging storage units from floor to ceiling. Add a shelf above the changing table or over a window, use a peg rack to hold coats or dresses, or attach metal bins to the wall to store toys or shoes.

Be creative when adding on-the-wall storage. Purchase ready-made wall accessories or search flea markets for old items to use in new ways. Nearly anything can be attached to the wall with screws or hook-and-loop tape.

Opposite: Turn a messy pile of picture books into a streamlined library with a magazine rack. Paint the piece to match the nursery. When wall space is dedicated to storage, find clever ways to display artwork. Here, a whimsical piece hangs from the ceiling.

Above: An antique piece with interesting shape and texture is attractive enough to double as art. This vintage shelf holds photos on its top ledge, while clothing graces its hooks.

Toddler Girls

Charm School

A little girl's room doesn't have to look childish. This sophisticated room could be mistaken for an adult guest room. The mixture of soft pattern and cottage style is a smart fit for a growing girl.

The grown-up look starts with cool colors. Creamy yellow and warm white coat the walls, which are punctuated with randomly painted cherries. White furniture is set off with pastel accessories.

Continue the classic design by showcasing salvaged furniture and fabrics, personal collections, and whimsical accents. Instead of pure perfection this room features an interesting mix of complementary pieces. For example, matching crystal knobs bind a variety of new and vintage pieces while the mismatched bed and bench look cohesive because of their similar size and shape.

Fabulous fabric puts the finishing touch on a shabby-chic room. Here multilayer treatments coordinate with the room's cottage look. New pink-and-white ticking side panels are topped with valances made from leftover nursery fabric. Above the bed's cozy quilt are framed quilt pieces and a double-fringed valance, creating an unusual canopy effect that mirrors the window treatments.

FOR INSTRUCTIONS ON MAKING A PICKET-FENCE BED, SEE PAGE 132.

Opposite: A traditional dressing table shares space along one wall with a curvy bench and a glass-front yellow chest with hinged, drop-down drawers. Cherries painted on the walls also appear on teacups stacked on two shelves and a diminutive footstool.

Above: Hanging the fabric treatments inside the window casing preserves the character that comes from the room's wide moldings.

Right: This room sports sunny color and vintage touches that complete a personal look. A picket-fence bed and cherries painted on the walls are key components to the style and charm of the space.

Room in Bloom

When a room's single, prominent window calls for more than a simple valance, sew curtain panels with a generous ruffle above the rod pocket to frame the view.

When you find something that you like, it can set the tone for the exact style and color of a room. This little girl's affinity for pink blossoms bloomed into a perennial bedroom that is comfortable and friendly.

Part of the charm of this bedroom is the lighthearted flower-stencil motif painted on the walls. Instead of being lined up in a border or arranged in a perfect grid, the flower motifs float around the room. After arranging the furniture, consciously position the flowers in a pleasing manner. Paint only portions of your motif above

windows and doors or have it pop out from behind a piece of furniture. Place the pattern imperfectly—it's more fanciful.

In a petite bedroom placing the furniture is the most difficult task. To avoid simply lining items up around the walls, position the bed at an angle. Try to arrange it so when you stand in the doorway you are looking from the foot to the head of the bed. This creates a more interesting layout and makes a room feel larger, much more so than walking into the side of a bed.

Above: Little girls love pretty pink rooms, but parents want spaces that will survive children's evolving tastes. Compromise with a floral fabric featuring plenty of pink but awash with other colors too.

FOR INSTRUCTIONS ON CREATING PAINTED POSIES, SEE PAGE 133.

Above: To contrast a room's curvaceous paint swirls and flowers, paint a soft check pattern with pink highlights on an armoire or dresser. Latex paint thinned with glaze achieves the transparent finish.

Right: Gently used furnishings complement the room's soft look. The old walnut dresser was rescued from a pile of castoffs destined for the dump. A fresh coat of paint and new knobs revive the tired piece.

To make the most of a cozy bedroom corner, paint a wall shelf and peg rack and use it to showcase treasures and hold jackets.

WELL-WORN STYLE
To give a piece of painted furniture new life with a well-worn and well-loved vintage look, follow these three steps.
1. Sand off old paint.
2. Rub a wax candle on edges and around pulls—wherever a weathered look is desired.
3. Brush on a fresh coat of paint. Lightly sand to remove the wax and reveal bare wood.

Above: Enjoy a summery bedroom all year with a fresh pastel scheme set by painted vintage furnishings. The tailored Roman shade balances the furniture's curves and blocks early-morning sunlight. A patchwork of floral prints dresses the bed.

Cottage Charm

Achieve a light, airy look in your little girl's room with the old-fashioned charm of vintage style. The cottage look offers a chance to mix and match favorite patterns and colors. It also creates a backdrop for heirlooms and flea market finds.

To achieve the cottage look, follow these easy, budget-friendly suggestions. Repaint and distress various pieces of furniture. Paint them and then sand the edges in various parts to give them a worn look. An heirloom iron bed anchors this room and is accented with new distressed pieces, such as the side table.

Flea markets and thrift shops are the ideal spots to find sturdy pieces to repaint for a child's room. Furnishings from the 1930s and 1940s are particularly good as they are well-made and often have simple, sophisticated shapes.

Top off the pretty scheme with a few well-chosen accessories. The new rag rug, vintage tole tray, and flea market linen sewn into a decorative pillow covering add to the cottage charm in this space. Straw hats on stands and hatboxes are playful finishing touches in a room designed to grow up with ease.

Always refinish and seal vintage pieces for safety.

Right: White paint and light distressing impart gentle wear to an old dressing table transformed into a desk that will work through the school years. A ruffled seat cushion adds a feminine accent.

Retro style in a little girl's bedroom can be both nostalgic and totally today. Bold colors and lots of geometric shapes make the mod look fun, while vintage and reproduction furnishings and accessories keep the room functional.

An energizing mix of bright colors—green, blue, yellow, pink, and orange—makes it clear that this isn't a sweet and frilly space. Dots and stripes give attitude, while a small dose of floral keeps the wilder patterns in check.

For the room's big-ticket items, stick with great basics—a white iron bed, white side table, and painted armoire. Furniture with wood finishes or white-painted pieces have a longer shelf life, changing easily from toddler to adult settings. They also convert quickly for guests by swapping out kids' sheets for more grown-up bedding.

Complete the throwback look with retro relics, including Kewpie dolls and an antique gum ball machine. Vintage pieces have stories that make them interesting. Keep the look here and now with modern shapes, such as a sleek red armchair and just-for-fun paper stars dangling overhead. Display your daughter's favorites but maintain order with a well-edited room.

Opposite: Let bedding lead the way. Here, concentric circles are mixed with bright stripes, florals, and large polka dots to create lovely layers any girl would adore. The patterns put a decidedly modern twist on a vintage color palette.

Top right: A cafe curtain is a cute nod to the past. This window treatment is made of a vintage tablecloth in a fun stylized floral.

Right: Store toys in old luggage, which is readily available at garage sales and flea markets, or reproduction pieces. The baggage is just right for underbed storage.

For funky flair skip matching accessories and go high contrast instead.

Fuchsia Frills

Pink may be the color of choice for a baby girl's nursery, but with a little planning it can survive into her teen years. Smart design in this room eliminates the fear of "here today, gone tomorrow."

When decorating for a child, even one whose mind changes weekly, don't forget the power of paint. Instead of sweet pastels this room uses two deep rosy hues for a look that will grow up with minor alterations. Hot pinks coupled with graphic designs give the room an energetic style. Orange and violet accents keep the look fresh and fun.

The bedding's grown-up mod flowers inspired the wall design. Mesh the playful flowers with other youthful accents, such as the pearl-studded neckroll pillow and sweet polka-dot sheers.

As your daughter grows, update the look quickly by switching in crisp white window treatments, a tailored bed skirt, and a few metal accessories. For a more dramatic change, add spice tones for a makeover with exotic flair that leaves the light pink behind.

Top right: Accent walls with a painted floral border created with a simple stencil and latex paint. When using a two-tone wall treatment put the lighter color on the top to give the room visual height.

Right: Dress up a simple bolster pillow with pretty trims. Hand-stitch rows of pearls, and add beaded tassels to the ends.

Opposite: Layers of colorful bedding pack a powerful punch in this girl's room. Mix and match solids and patterns to make the bed the center of attention.

Large floor pillows invite
friends to get comfy.

Color Happy

Even on cloudy days this girl's bedroom seems sunny, thanks to its citrus hues and whimsical style. Whitewashed surfaces, colorful furnishings, and simple patterns create a snappy, comfy look that combines country simplicity with modern attitude.

The fun and fruity look starts with a bright green and purple color scheme. Take your color cues from nature—lime and grape are a perfect pair. When using a rainbow of colors, be sure they are all the same intensity or brightness.

Bright colors are even more interesting when paired with large expanses of negative space. Paint the walls, ceiling, doors, and moldings white to create a blank canvas for the cacophony of color. White gives the eye visual breathing space, making a room seem larger. Plus a white room is a blank slate that can be redecorated as a child's tastes change.

Painted furniture is a fun way to introduce color and add character without overwhelming a room. The pieces can be stripped and repainted later if her tastes change. Pay attention to scale when choosing furnishings and accessories.

Opposite: So color collects at more than one level, employ the palette high and low. In this room paper-globe lights add a shot of citrus closer to the ceiling, while a rainbow-stripe rug brings color underfoot. A lime green bed frame and linens in purple stripes and solids brighten the space in between.

Right: A secondhand vanity gets a whole new attitude with a coat of lime green paint. Orange polka dots add a playful touch to the purple-painted stool.

Layering a variety of bedding or accessories distracts and disguises flawed furniture.

COLOR CUES

Color is often the inspiration for a decorating scheme, but with so many choices it can be difficult to know where to start.

• Let paint manufacturers' paint chips guide you. Choose colors of the same tone—intensity or degree of lightness or darkness—by picking hues located in the same space on different cards.

• Look at the color wheel. Create an eye-pleasing palette with complementary colors—those that are opposite one another on the wheel—such as blue and orange or green and purple.

Jungle Fever

Looking to add a little wow to your kid's room? Use bold colors and a fun-filled theme to transform a boring bedroom into a tropical paradise. Choose an inspiration piece to start your design. A bedspread by designer Lilly Pulitzer was the jumping-off point for this cheerful and colorful space.

Although conventional wisdom might dictate leaving the walls in a small bedroom white, rich color and a bold mural actually serve to enlarge this tiny space (the white ceiling provides visual relief and a feeling of height). Start with a base coat of satin or semigloss paint; flat paint will bleed. Add a menagerie of monkeys, flamingos, parrots, and palm trees. If drawing isn't your forte, use stencils or trace images projected onto the wall.

Carry the "beachy keen" tropical theme throughout the room with furniture and accessories. A cabana is like a private indoor fort where your child can read, draw, or hide from a sneaky sibling.

Vibrant discount-store rugs in various shapes and sizes are a great alternative to expensive and hard-to-clean wall-to-wall carpeting. Layer them for a rainbow effect that is gentle on little feet and holds up to boom-box boogying. Double-sided tape keeps the rugs from sliding.

Use remnant fabrics to make the lampshade covers and other accessories; create perky bed pillows with loads of by-the-yard ball fringe. You can sew on the trims or use a hot-glue gun. Embellish a solid-color bed skirt with other scraps or outgrown clothing and sew on rickrack and ball fringe using a zigzag stitch.

Treat closets as part of the wall space when painting a mural. Continuing the design over the doors will maximize space and make the room look larger than its actual dimensions.

FOR INSTRUCTIONS ON MAKING A COOL CABANA, SEE PAGE 134.

Opposite: Anyone handy with a jigsaw can make a perky cutout palm tree headboard. Cut a simple shape from inexpensive 3/4-inch fiberboard, which is thicker and stronger than plywood and adds needed dimension to the wall's flat expanse. Paint the finished design and add a coat of varnish to protect it from scratches and other kid-style shenanigans.

Above: Create a handy, sandy surprise from a stock end table. Add a layer of sand, toys, and some sporty shades on a painted end table (look for one with finials) and cover it with a 3/4-inch-thick piece of glass.

Right: Fanciful window treatments in green and yellow provide a visual break from the expanse of pink in this bedroom. Transform an old radiator cover into a pretty perch. Cover cut-to-size foam with bright fabric and coordinating piping and attach the skirt to the cover using hook-and-loop tape.

FOR INSTRUCTIONS ON MAKING THE
WINDOW SHADE, SEE PAGE 135.

Two by Two

When two girls share one small room, things can get chaotic. Help your daughters save their relationship by letting them stake out personal space and teaching them to share other areas.

Ask the girls to pick a paint color on which they both can agree. Bright green walls provide a great backdrop for all things colorful. Give each girl a matching sleeping station, separated by an easy-to-spot rug. Have the children express their creativity by crafting their own artwork and accessories.

With supervision your girls can make pillows, window treatments, and even a bucket lampshade (just drill a hole in the bottom of the bucket to accommodate a finial). To make bold artwork, tear tissue paper in various colors and decoupage the pieces to artist's canvas using all-purpose glue. The girls can create flowers or more abstract designs.

If the small room lacks the space for two bedside tables, encourage the girls to share a wide medical cabinet. An auto body shop painter can give the metal a super shiny finish. The girls also may need to share one workspace. Cleaning out a closet to make room for such a space is well worth the sacrifice, especially in a room for kids.

Opposite: Symmetry in a shared room can prevent disputes about who has the nicer place to lounge. Use a bold runner on an area rug to divide the room and define the separate spaces.

Above: In a bedroom with multiple closets, converting one into a work area is a smart use of space. To make it work make sure everything is removable, including the desk and shelves, so the closet can be reclaimed if needed.

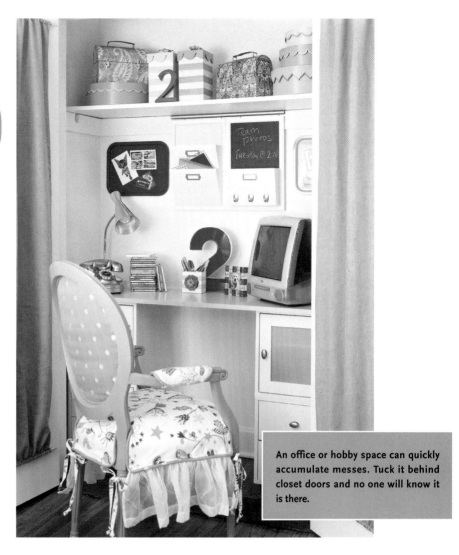

An office or hobby space can quickly accumulate messes. Tuck it behind closet doors and no one will know it is there.

WALL TREAT
Don't overlook a narrow slice of wall. With a bit of imagination, the area can become a focal point. This vine of flowers grows up the wall and around a matching armchair. Take your cues for the design from patterns in the room's bedding or accessories.
• Trace bits of the pattern onto paper and enlarge or reduce the design as desired using a copy machine.
• Trace the final patterns onto acrylic sheets and cut out the design with a crafts knife. Use this stencil and crafts paint to add the design to the wall.
• Finish the look by adding the motif to a chair back. Scan the design on your computer and print it on transfer paper or ask a copy shop to do the same. Once the motif is on transfer paper, iron it onto the fabric following the manufacturer's instructions.

Sibling Revelry

Put any three girls in the same bedroom and you can expect territorial disputes, squabbles over toys, and identity crises. Wage peace with a pretty-in-pastel retreat that clearly gives each girl her domain.

For individuality each of these big, chunky beds is dressed slightly differently in a mix of florals, stripes, and ruffles. The look is unified with identical pink coverlets and floral shams.

Pink and flowers are certainly sweet, but this room is far from saccharine. The biggest jolt of color is the yellow that splashes the upper walls; pink plays only a supporting role—a cheerful solution for girls who are still growing and for busy parents who may lack the time to redo the room when the pink phase passes. Scallop-edge painted furnishings coupled with accessories unearthed at antiques stores also lend a more mature look.

Function is important too. Hatboxes provide storage with style, while the fabric-lined baskets on a shelving unit are easy to retrieve. The result is a room where three little girls can go for some quiet time, relaxation, fun, and enjoyment for many years to come.

Right: New white wainscoting gives this room cottage charm and provides a clean backdrop for lavender furniture. The scallop detailing on the wood furniture is echoed on the pink coverlets and wicker basket liners.

Below: Painted flower-shape pegs beside the dresser are hung at the perfect height for the girls to reach their necklaces, purses, and other belongings. Wood letters propped on the ledge above coordinate with the pegs.

Hidden Treasures

In a growing girl's room, especially one belong to a girl with an extensive wardrobe, closet space is prime real estate. It may be necessary to find other space in the room to stash away toys, clothes, games, and more.

If all that stuff remains visible, however, it can look like clutter. No one likes a messy room, especially Mom, so lose the litter with a clever trick. Use skirts and panels to create storage space that's easy to access and just as easy to hide.

Be inventive with fabric curtains. You can use them almost anywhere to maximize the room's storage space. Easy-to-construct panels can capture unused areas under a desk or bed, on shelves, or in an open-front armoire or chest. Skirts keep the area well hidden at all times, while panels can be closed to hide clutter or pulled back with ties to reveal what is behind.

Left: Put a fresh coat of paint on an old set of bookshelves and add curtains inside with hook-and-loop tape. Pretty ribbon tiebacks make the panels look as attractive open as they do closed.

SEW GOOD
Even a novice seamstress can create simple fabric panels. Measure the space you'll be masking and cut the fabric to the desired size (double the width if you want a pleated look). Hem the sides and sew rod pockets across the top and bottom. Make sure the pockets are large enough to accommodate the dowel or tension rod from which the panels will hang. Thread the rod through the pockets and hang your creation in place. If you choose a tension rod, simply snap or twist it into place. If you use a wood dowel, secure it with eye hooks screwed into the door or shelves.

Left: Replace the glass fronts of a small chest with fabric panels for out-of-sight storage.

Below left: A bed skirt is always a wise choice in a kid's room. The inexpensive item allows the floor space beneath the bed to be used to hide bins containing off-season clothes.

Below right: A skirted dressing table smartly camouflages storage behind its ruffles.

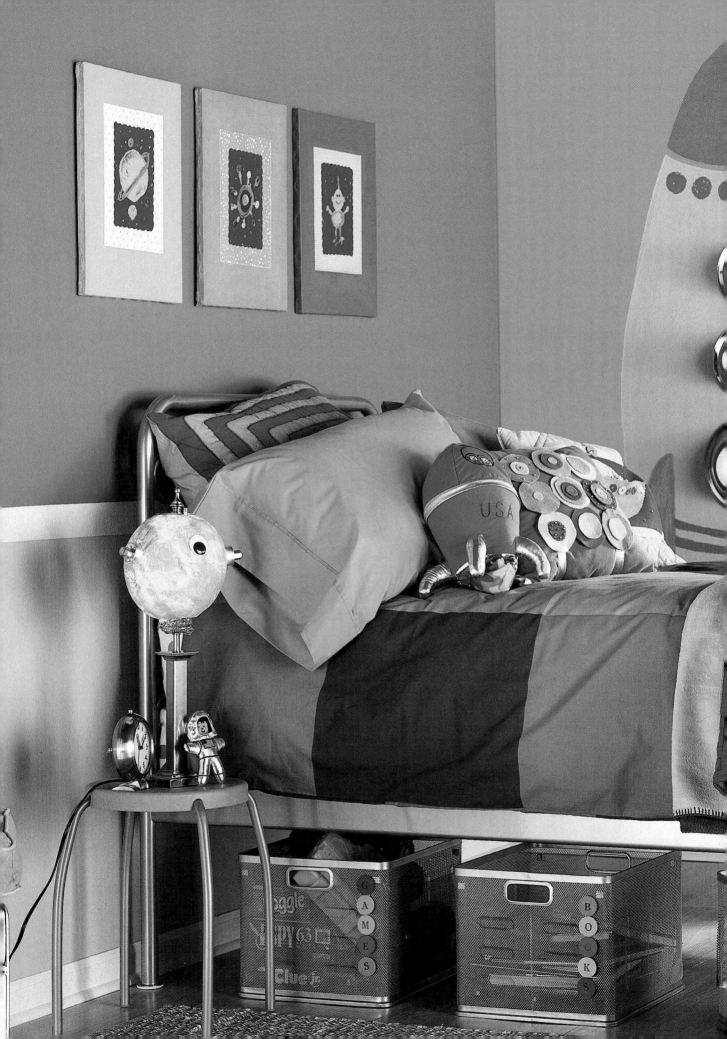

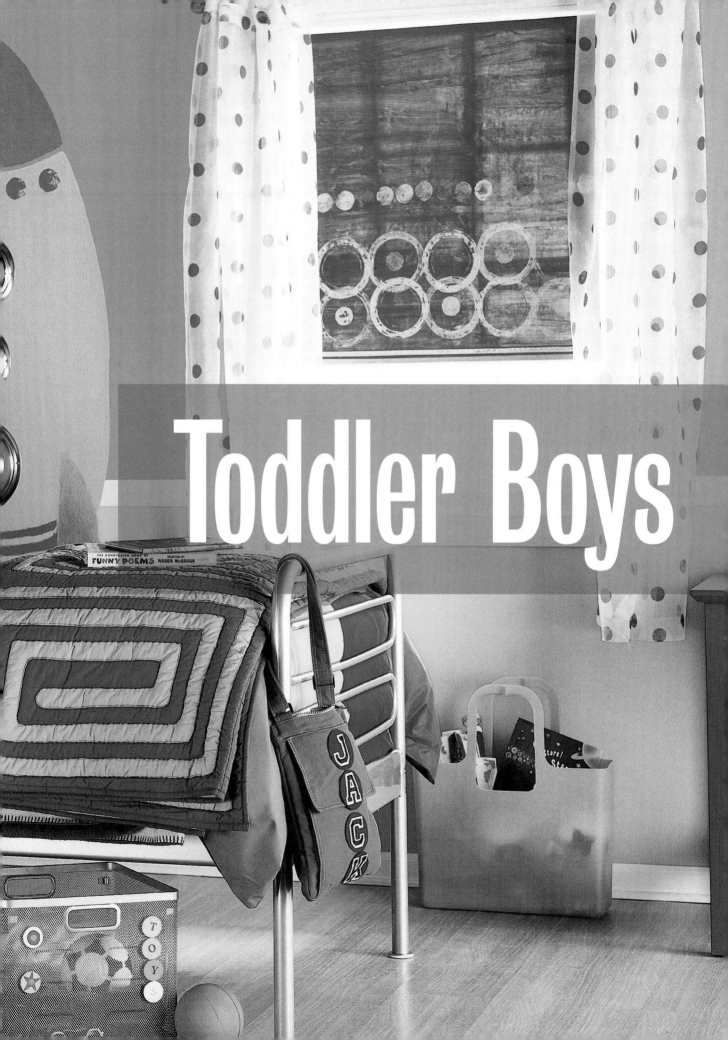

Toddler Boys

A neutral color scheme makes this bedroom as interesting as any juvenile room but more sophisticated.

Neutral Knockout

Who says you can't create a boy's room that will grow with him? This room's neutral palette and ageless design will serve its occupant's needs for years to come. The scheme is built upon a generic background and finished with simple furniture and accessories.

A neutral base doesn't have to be beige—it can be any foundation color that works with accessories that speak to a child's interests. In this room a brown and green scheme ties in nicely with a love of nature. Smaller details acknowledge the theme, including animal-shape lamp

bases, a pinecone motif on the dresser mirror, and antlers above the desk.

Striped wallpaper and a mix of plaid fabrics further emphasize the cabin look. The patterns also add color and motion, proving that a room with a neutral base doesn't have to be boring. More interest comes from a duvet cover, slipcovered chair and ottoman, and fabric valances.

The room's suite of furniture is void of age-specific designs and colors. Instead the numerous wood pieces have simple appeal that will persist through the years. A twin bed frees up floor space for the

chair and ottoman, which provide a spot to read or hang out with friends. The bed's trundle is handy for sleepovers.

Above: Two different finishes showcase the room's many wood furnishings. The natural wood tones give the room warmth, while a green stain applied in a streaky wash adds color and textural interest.

Opposite: Three furniture pieces form a wall of function. The desk is deep enough to accommodate a computer, while the bookshelves provide display space.

ON DISPLAY

Children love their collections—and those treasured items can quickly get out of control. When decorating a kid's room, make a list (with measurements) of all collectibles and think about how you will display or store them. The process is time-consuming, but the results of less mess and clutter are well worth it.

This room's occupant is an avid collector of sports items. Wall-mounted shelves and pegs hold trophies, pictures, and hats; shallow ledges display sports cards. Shelves flanking the desk hold books and memorabilia, while cabinets and drawers below store games.

Retro Reinvented

room 1940s boy-and-dog calendar prints sparked the color scheme—mossy green walls and rich terra-cotta accents.

Left: Shelves at the head and foot of the bed keep bedtime stories close at hand. They also add much-needed storage space to a one-closet bedroom.

Below: Decoupage can revive a slightly battered dresser or create interest on new furnishings. This small dresser features a map-motif treatment. The piece received a coat of gold paint, and the drawer fronts were covered with color copies of pages from a world atlas.

Opposite: A plywood built-in bed framed by an arched cutout provides more than a stylish sleeping space. It also acts as hideout, sailboat, and theater.

Timeless, sophisticated midcentury style is perfect for a growing boy's room. The era's warm, faded hues may be an unexpected choice, but they are a smart starting point for a design with staying power. Create a nostalgic space that will please your senses and nurture his love of adventure and exploration.

Save floor space and provide a strong focal point with a snug Pullman-car-style built-in bed. Constructed of ¾-inch plywood, the structure occupies the entire window wall of the room. The arched opening creates an alcove that makes the bed feel like its own room. The bed serves as everything from stage to boat.

The cozy bed also offers additional storage space in a room with just one small closet. Drawers in the base of the unit are perfect for stowing games, toys, and puzzles. Shelves at the foot and head of the bed add display space. Tall cabinets flanking the arch are good for larger items, such as ball bats.

Search flea markets for vintage prints to serve as inspiration for a room. In this

Use matching frames and mats to unify prints that vary in size.

Custom Creation

An energy-packed color palette of blue, red, and yellow coupled with bold geometric patterns creates a timeless room that feels boyish yet will grow with the child. Achieve the look without spending a fortune by using paint to refurbish old pieces of furniture.

Go crazy with pattern. March checks across the chairs and desks, deck out dressers and headboards with columns of stripes, and use the nonbusiness end of a paintbrush to create tiny dots on chair legs and mirrors. Repeat the geometric theme in the room's linens.

Balance the bold designs of the furnishings with calm walls. Use a mixture of glaze and paint to create a softly textured wall treatment. A subtle harlequin pattern on one wall picks up on the room's angles and helps to visually foreshorten a long and narrow room.

Position beds back-to-back along one wall in the room to leave the rest of the floor space open for playtime. Add desks for homework, set up a table and chairs for art projects or games, and provide painted pails for neatly stashing away toys. Complete the look by displaying vintage toys on window ledges or on wall and above-door shelves.

Opposite: Pay attention to even the smallest accent pieces in a room. A few touches of paint can quickly give a trash can, corkboard, and lamp base a coordinated look.

Above left and right: Clever use of paint and pattern can make mismatched flea market finds look like a coordinated set.

Above right: Create a custom bed skirt by sewing triangle flags onto a sheet.

FURNITURE FIX-UP

Use paint to customize a piece of furniture to match any decor. New unfinished or sturdy vintage wood pieces are easiest to paint.

• Materials: Choose high-quality paints that will adhere well to the primed surface. In general latex enamel paints work best for painting furnishings. Also use good brushes and keep brushstrokes to a minimum to avoid streaks.

• Preparation: Lightly sand the piece and wipe with a tack cloth to remove dust. Cover the piece with primer tinted the same color as the base coat. If the piece was painted before, use paint stripper to remove old layers of paint or sand the piece to create a smooth finish before adding primer and paint.

• Painting: Apply two or more thin coats of paint, allowing each to dry thoroughly between coats. When dry apply any desired accent colors or patterns.

• Finishing: Seal the completed piece with several coats of water-base polyurethane to protect it from wear and tear.

Game On

Score points with your little basketball fanatic by turning his bedroom into a miniature gymnasium, complete with a hoop. With careful planning and a bit of creativity, a sports-theme room can put the "fun" in functional.

The design starts with a laminate plank floor to mimic the look of a wooden basketball court and tape to create the key. The furniture is positioned along the perimeter of the room, leaving plenty of space for play in the middle. A soft version of a basketball makes indoor play safer and quieter.

Bright blue storage lockers flank a simple shelving unit, creating a wall

You'll get the best results when you play off kids' personalities and work with them for a unique look.

Below: A bench in the walk-in closet continues the look of a locker room and provides a handy spot where kids can sit down and put on shoes. Plenty of cubbyholes keep abundant shoes and hats organized.

of sporty storage—the perfect place to display well-earned trophies and a collection of autographed balls, photos, and other memorabilia.

A kid's room is where you should have fun with accessories and paint. In this space decorative painting gives the walls a gymnasium look with the impression of old brick with peeling plaster. Pendent lighting fixtures—just like ones found in a gym—hang from the bedroom ceiling.

Opposite: Kids love color and thematic details, and this room delivers both. From the flooring to the walls, no detail is overlooked.

Above: A few special touches help an ordinary computer desk fit the sporting theme. Real baseballs are drilled and screwed to the drawers as playful pulls. Tracks secured to a black-painted plywood valance transform it into the scoreboard. Letters and numbers cut from melamine keep score.

Fast Lane

Give your little road warrior the room of his dreams. A boy who has a knack for identifying the make and model of any car he sees surely will give the green light to this theme, an auto lover's dream.

Treat the walls to a streetwise design. First cover them in an easy-to-clean blue semigloss paint. Cover the blue with chalkboard paint and let it dry. (The paint goes on brown but dries gray.) Add yellow semigloss road divider lines. Start with one horizontal road spanning the entire room at chair-rail height (about 36 to 40 inches high). Add vertical roads branching off the main road.

Primary colors are the foundation of this room, but the addition of black and white lends a racetrack zip. Unify disparate furniture pieces with similar paint treatments. Sand down thrift store furnishings, such as this room's desk, and

SHADE OF LIGHT

To make adjustable window shades, sew simple panels from checkerboard fabric lined with black. The panels have top and bottom rod pockets; the top one holds a tension rod, and the bottom one holds a dowel, which helps the shade hang flat and makes it easier to roll up. Each tie is a single long strand of red ribbon, secured with thread at the top of the shade. To raise the shade, simply roll up the bottom and tie the ribbons.

Shiny toy cars make fun, sculptural accessories in a boy's room. Hang them from nails on the walls so they appear to be driving on the roads.

apply acrylic paint using all the room's colors. Or purchase new unfinished items and dress them up in red with black and white accents.

Fill out the room with traffic-related accessories. The checkerboard pattern on the window shades and chair cushion looks like a race flag; the pattern repeats on the desk and dresser drawers as well as the mirror frame and switchplate.

Opposite: The simplest route to an automobile theme is filling a room with stock and custom accessories. A kids' catalog proved fruitful for finding the parking-meter piggy bank, traffic light, and detour sign. The road signs are reproductions from a local antiques mall.

Above: Encourage tidiness by giving your child plenty of storage space. This dresser offers deep drawers for clothes as well as all those toy cars.

Left: Put a hand-me-down desk back in the fast lane with a bright makeover. Sand down the old finish and revive the piece with splashes of primary colors.

Space Odyssey

Give your budding astronaut a memorable bedroom that's clearly out of this world. He'll blast off to dreamland in a room dotted with aliens, spacecraft, and new-tech accessories.

The surest way to get your son's approval for the room is to get him involved in decorating it. This space-age space features plenty of colorful accessories he can craft. Send a simple window shade into orbit with stamped motifs and finish the treatment with atomic finials made from multicolor plastic-foam balls. Pile the bed with colorful linens and plain pillows dressed up with easy-to-glue felt designs.

Create a galaxy of fun by adding interactive elements to the design. Paint a simple rocket shape on the wall and add touch lights to simulate liftoff. Help your little boy transmit messages to earthlings with a pile of painted alphabet rocks.

Set up a communications base to serve as mission control (and, of course,

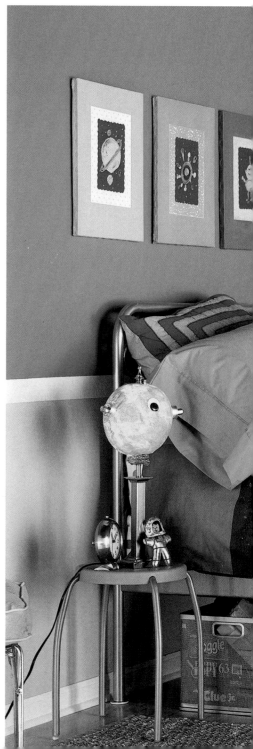

a desk for homework). Create a message center by attaching cork circles to the wall with removable mounting stickers. For intergalactic signals add magnets to wooden disks.

Find lots of space-related games and art projects on NASA's kids' site, www.nasa.gov/audience/forkids/home/index.html

Opposite: Encourage your child's love of math and science with a colorful space-theme workstation. Hang posters of astronaut role models, load the desk with sci-fi accessories, and let his imagination zoom into orbit.

Below: This far-out room will transport your child to the farthest corners of the cosmos. Let him express his creativity with outer-space art made with decoupage and paint or a papier-mâché treatment that uses tissue paper to turn an ordinary lamp "alien."

Hunt for easy-to-adapt furniture pieces at hardware, office, and kitchen supply stores or at tag sales.

Opposite: An ordinary wood bed looks cool topped with a fleece spread in deep colors and pillows in stripes and plaids. Above the bed a rack and hooks made for undercabinet use hold caps and vintage bowling pins.

Left: This wood desk is enriched with a deep navy stain then outfitted with funky steel accessories, including a chair, a garbage pail, and shelving.

Below: An old filing cabinet, dragged out of a basement, is repainted to serve as a unique dresser. On top a striped cylinder lampshade adds color.

Winning Look

A room with a hip collegiate feel will keep a young boy happy well into his teen years. Start with great wall color, add lots of rough-and-tumble furnishings, and finish by dropping in cool materials and accessories with tons of texture.

The muted yellow-cast green on the walls is a terrific neutral backdrop for a striped wall treatment reminiscent of old rugby shirts. Multiwidth bands of old gold, navy, and burgundy painted just above the baseboard anchor and energize the room. Although furniture blocks some of the stripes, what is visible is more than enough to give the room a sense of youthful fun.

Add a masculine edge by adapting unlikely pieces. In this room a metal filing cabinet is repainted and used as a dresser (perfect for stowing bulky sweaters),

while hanging bins meant to hold utensils and spice bottles adapt to corral pencils. Other fun ideas include using a metal tool chest to hold desk supplies and storing books in bins.

When the wall treatment and furniture are in place, give the room texture. Use metal and wood pieces to provide sleep, work, and storage solutions. Soften the look with fleece on the bed, corduroy on thick-fringed flap pillows, sisal carpet, and a red faux-fur rug. Tap into vintage colors and motifs to create a winning boy's room.

Overlapping green "hills" are stitched onto red pillow shams and along the bottom half of a blue fleece throw to mimic the wallpaper's farm-field pattern.

Red is used on furnishings, a closet-covering fabric panel, and window treatments to create a cheery setting. The primary color scheme is stimulating for a young child. Along with smart looks the room boasts savvy function. Bunk beds preserve floor space, and a wall of built-in shelving adds loads of storage space.

Left: Paint an unfinished dresser to match the room's barn door and pull out the red in the wallpaper. Painted drawer pulls complement the room's table and chairs.

Below: Climbing up and down a bunk bed ladder can provide hours of fun for growing brothers. The space-saving sleeping arrangement is also practical in a small bedroom that must be shared by two rambunctious boys.

Opposite: Think outside the box when decorating a small bedroom. By removing closet doors and narrowing the closet opening by 6 inches, the room has enough space for a window seat and oodles of built-in shelves and cubbies that stretch to the ceiling.

Farmhouse Fun

Cultivate plans for a farmhouse bedroom that's acres of fun for a pair of growing boys. A theme room can be both fun and functional—a play space and bedroom that can grow with the boys. It also can stand the test of time, as a few small changes can take the room from toddler to tween years.

The bright red barn-style door makes the room's theme loud and clear. Behind the door is a dramatic wall treatment. Farm-theme wallpaper featuring rolling green hills is placed on the wall opposite the bunk beds. The other walls are painted a buttery yellow pulled from the tiny houses in the paper's design. No worries if the boys outgrow the motif—new wallpapers are easy to remove.

Simple seamstress work helps tie the bedding into the room's theme.

Promote reading by storing favorite books at your child's eye level on a low shelf or in a hanging basket.

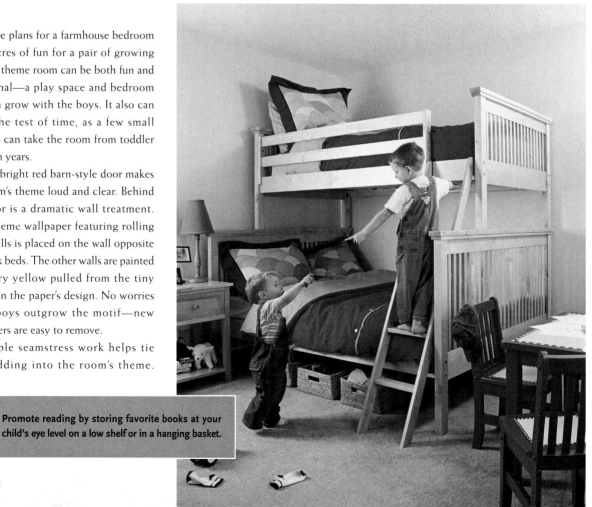

A room for two means two of most things, so look for bargain fabrics, inexpensive furniture you can repaint, and window treatments you can make yourself.

Wild West

Two brothers bunking up in one bedroom? No problem. A Western motif is timeless and charming—perfect for two little cowboys. Get the look with a variety of garage sale finds, thematic fabrics, and simple decorating techniques.

Begin by pulling a color palette from an inspiration fabric or piece of art. In this room a cowboy-motif pillow spurred the red, beige, and blue scheme. Key elements—wall paint, flooring, furnishings, and window treatments—are kept unembellished so the room can grow with the boys. Straw-hue walls and denim curtains are timeless choices.

Drive home the theme with easy-to-change bedding and other accessories. Cover the bed in bandana-inspired linens and Western-print pillows. Put a cactus cutout on display, scatter child-size cowboy boots and hats throughout the room, and search online and in thrift shops for Wild West artwork and knickknacks. The boys will get into the spirit of the room, playing with all the cowboy gear.

In this shared room the boys sleep side by side in twin beds. Let each child express his individuality by allowing him to select his own bedding, above-bed artwork, and other accessories.

Opposite: Two little buckaroos sack up in this red and blue dude ranch. Its crowning achievement is a ledge perfect for corralling clutter and displaying cowboy collections.

Below: Search for a few fun elements that really play up the room's theme.

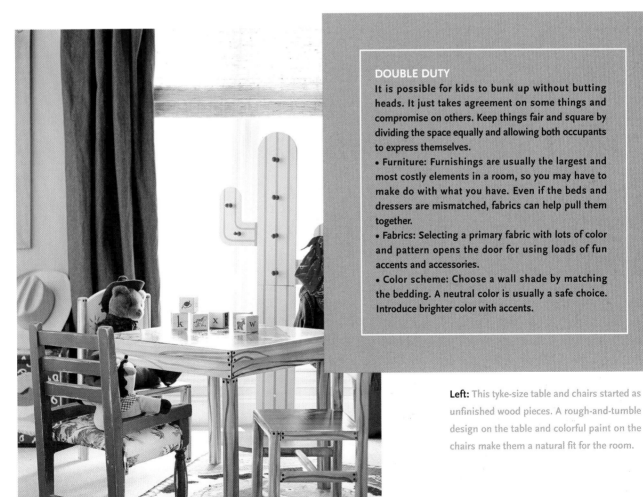

DOUBLE DUTY

It is possible for kids to bunk up without butting heads. It just takes agreement on some things and compromise on others. Keep things fair and square by dividing the space equally and allowing both occupants to express themselves.

• Furniture: Furnishings are usually the largest and most costly elements in a room, so you may have to make do with what you have. Even if the beds and dressers are mismatched, fabrics can help pull them together.

• Fabrics: Selecting a primary fabric with lots of color and pattern opens the door for using loads of fun accents and accessories.

• Color scheme: Choose a wall shade by matching the bedding. A neutral color is usually a safe choice. Introduce brighter color with accents.

Left: This tyke-size table and chairs started as unfinished wood pieces. A rough-and-tumble design on the table and colorful paint on the chairs make them a natural fit for the room.

Custom Look

Older homes are often filled with interesting architectural details, including built-in units. If your home lacks ready-made storage, adding custom-built creations can be costly. Get a similar look without the hefty price tag with off-the-shelf pieces that fit the room's look.

Case goods (another name for storage furniture) include freestanding furniture that allows for flexible arrangement and modular systems that include separate, coordinated units. When purchasing new cabinetry measure the space you want to fill to find the appropriate piece.

Get creative with stock cabinetry to fashion a custom look in your son's room. Flank a window with tall bookshelves, use modular shelving as a room divider, mount storage cubes on the wall, or put casters on old dresser drawers for attractive underbed storage. Use storage units along the walls to leave open floor space where toddlers can play.

Above right: A bench placed under a window is an ideal daydreaming spot for your tot. The open spaces below provide handy storage, and the cushion is easy to replace as he grows and his taste changes.

Right: Bookshelves keep books and toys visible yet store things close to the floor where toddlers play. Hang a large piece of art above the bookshelves to make them feel more substantial and paint them to coordinate with the room's color scheme.

Opposite: School lockers are a playful and hardworking choice for a child's room. This bold unit introduces kid-friendly colors and creates several spots for stashing stuff.

They don't make furniture like they used to, so shopping secondhand is sometimes the best way to find quality wood pieces.

STORAGE SAFETY

• Invest in well-made pieces. Check sturdiness and be certain the hinges and supports are strong.

• New furniture designed specifically for children is risk free as it meets the standards set by the Juvenile Products Manufacturers Association and the Consumer Products Safety Commission. If you purchase antiques or new furnishings designed for adults, look for sharp edges that can cause injury or removable pieces that could lead to choking.

• All storage units, regardless of how stable they appear, should be bolted or bracketed securely to the walls. Also, place heavier items on bottom shelves.

• Put desirable toys in floor bins or on low shelves to discourage climbing.

• Hang shelves high enough to prevent a child from using them as a jungle gym.

• If you use a toy box or trunk for storage, make sure it operates with safety hinges. You can retrofit any item to include this safety measure.

Teens

Hipster Hangout

Load a bed with fabrics that include a mix of stylized patterns and textures—from faux fur to polished cottons edged with glass beads.

Repetition of color, pattern, and texture is the key to creating unity.

Light Side

As your daughter inches toward adulthood, create an atmosphere in her bedroom that is soft and feminine with a youthful twist. Pretty pastels splash this room with personality, while homey fabrics keep the small space light and airy.

A queen-size bed that monopolizes the room is the obvious focal point. It becomes a showstopper with lovely layers of vintage-style bedding. A white-on-white polka-dot sheer forms a top-layer duvet cover, which is sewn a little larger than the striped cover beneath.

The bed skirt incorporates the same sheer fabric alternating with patterned fabric rectangles. The skirt's banding, made from raspberry fabric, acts as a frame for the bedding ensemble. The skirt attaches to muslin, which lies between the box spring and mattress. The bed is topped with cute-as-a-button custom pillows that feature unexpected embellishments, including pockets fashioned from kitschy tropical fabric.

Antique accents, including side tables and an armoire, give the room soul. The painted furnishings add fresh flavor and define a cottage style, while vintage accessories make the room look like it has been evolving for years.

Above right: Plastic buttons hot-glued to a wooden picture frame give this feminine room jewel-like detail. Use a collection of new buttons or try vintage buttons or beads for a similar look.

Right: Get your teen involved in making decorative pillows for her bed. For this button pillow sew ribbon in a lattice pattern on an insert panel; accent the intersections with buttons. Miter gingham strips at the corners for the panel's frame and finish with piping.

Opposite: Mix large and small sheers, stripes, and tiny prints in livable pastels for an eye-opening design. When traditional nightstands are too big, narrow side tables

Livable pastels punch up the room's style and make for light rest.

ACCENTUATE THE POSITIVE

Casual accents create a relaxed attitude. Play with paint for these quick style solutions.

• Furniture fix-ups: Rather than buying new furniture, give existing pieces a fresh update with paint. An armoire sports lime green, while side tables brighten up with red.

• Adaptable accents: A thrifty picture frame finds new character with paint and button embellishments. Wood office bins from a discount store get new coats of pastel paint and are tucked in the armoire to keep things organized.

Pump Up the Volume

If your daughters prefer cool and fun to cute and frilly, go for a color scheme that's bold and eye-catching. A teen's room can be treated differently than more traditional rooms in the house and should reflect the child's personality.

Use lime green walls as a bright backdrop for hip-hued fabrics. The bedding and curtains in this room use hot-hot pink and pumped-up purple in solids and stripes.

Tent-style enclosures define and crown each bed. The canopies provide a cocoon of privacy that makes each girl feel snug in her own space. Rod pockets were sewn in the center of the canopies and slipped over wrought-iron rods suspended just below ceiling height. Coordinating sheer treatments also dangle from swing-arm rods at the windows.

For dimension and flexibility sew two fabrics together to make each canopy reversible (pick a fabric with a soft drape that won't pucker). Use a complementary stripe as a tailored bed skirt, which can hide underbed storage. High headboards stop the tall canopies from dwarfing the twin beds. Above them striped frames give botanical prints a funky facelift.

Opposite: Clever canopies help set beds apart—and may even reduce quarrels—in a shared room. Go for symmetry with matching fabrics and wall art or let each girl choose different (yet harmonious) patterns and colors to express her personal style.

Right: Suspended on wing rods well above the window, double-sided panels open and close like shutters, revealing purple fabric on one side and a pink-on-pink stripe on the other. The panels make the windows appear longer and nicely frame vivacious art.

Keep the design simple, clean, durable, and washable. In other words, make it teen-friendly.

Star-Spangled Style

A red, white, and blue color scheme is a classic choice that never goes out of style.

When decorating for an All-American boy, you can't go wrong with red, white, and blue. Boys quickly grow into young men, and an Americana theme will age well. Start with basic white walls and simple wood furnishings and choose fun accessories that can be changed little by little as your son gets older.

White walls can do amazing things for a space—it is like letting the sun in to wash the room with light. Contrast the crisp walls with a painted ceiling. A touch of deep blue above creates the feeling of the sky; add yellow stars for a night reminiscent of a campout.

Rustic furniture and accessories rule this roost. A mix of handmade, flea market, and new furniture keeps the look interesting. The new bed frame is suitable for a young boy or a tall teen and can shift to a guest room later. An old-school desk stained a deep ebony adds warmth and

maturity. A twig side table—still popular in Adirondack camps today—holds a collection of CDs.

Fill the space with loads of red, white, and blue decorative elements—everything from cotton rugs and throw pillows to picture frames and folk art. Exercise your freedom to mix patterns, including Old Glory-inspired stars and stripes.

Left: The Craftsman-style bed is covered with a simple, cushy white coverlet. Striped pillows in red and blue add color, while a lace-up pillowcase provides visual interest and a decidedly masculine touch. A primitive ladder serves as a place to hang extra blankets during sleepovers.

Below: A blue and white slipcovered armchair offers a comfy spot to relax and read. A handmade bulletin board showcases photos of friends and family.

HIPPIES
—USE—→
SIDE DOOR

Left: A rolling modular storage unit curbs clutter and provides a spot for tunes, trophies, and other teen stuff.

Below: Black chalkboard paint is a great idea for a teen who likes to doodle, jot down friends' phone numbers, or play hangman with friends. Mom can use it to remind him to clean his room or study for a test.

Opposite: The techno-style metal bed is piled high with eye-popping pillows featuring squiggles, stars, sunbursts, and other spunky patterns that lighten up the black room.

Mod Squad

Every mom dreads the day her son asks to paint his room black. Worry no more. This supercool room proves that a dark space need not look like a dungeon. Encourage his self-expression—and keep your sanity—with a retro-inspired room that uses black paint and accessories in small doses.

This kid- and parent-friendly bedroom uses black chalkboard paint on the top portion of the walls. Below the dark color is a bright and cheery hue: a serene sky blue. Other vibrant hues—including

purple and teal—would pair equally well with black.

Sleek and simple accessories complete the crisp decor. Sophisticated furniture, such as the three-tier glass table and metal bed, can later make an easy transition to dorm room, guest room, or first apartment. Funky bedding and punchy green Roman shades keep the space fun and youthful.

An inexpensive metal chair rail frames the space and provides a handy spot for posters and other teen treasures displayed with vintage or souvenir magnets. Made of 4-foot metal strips from a home improvement store, the chair rail is screwed into the wall. The exposed screws add to the look.

USING BLACK PAINT

Help your nonconformist teen feel special (and make a statement everyone can live with) by saying yes to black, at least in small doses. Encourage self-expression and keep your sanity with these tips for using black paint with success:

• Dark colors can feel confining. Lighten up in a small bedroom and skip black on a ceiling, as it will make it appear lower. Black is a great accent, especially when paired with silver in an outer-space or starry-night theme.

• Afraid to use black on the walls? A coat of black paint is a good, thrifty way to update juvenile or hand-me-down furniture for a teen's room. Black furniture is becoming as popular as white furniture in the juvenile market.

• Stay away from shiny black paint. The shinier the paint, the more wall imperfections show. For both scrubbability and style, look for a satin finish or one of the new washable flat paints on the market.

FOR INSTRUCTIONS ON MAKING A
MOLDING CANOPY, SEE PAGE 136.

Old-School Cool

Use funky flea market finds to design a hip and cozy retreat for your son. Vintage shops offer inexpensive furnishings and accessories, so you won't be disappointed if he spills soda on his new desk or accidentally breaks a knob on the dresser.

When decorating your teen's room, look beyond the usual places to find what you need. Scour yard sales and thrift stores for chairs, chests, trunks, and other furniture that you can make over with daring paint colors and cool hardware.

Look at the potential of every old item you see. Antique glass jars, once used for canning, make fun pencil holders. A metal chicken feeder is just the right width to hold rulers, erasers, and pushpins on a desktop. Wooden pallets that once held plants at a nursery can be used to store blankets at the foot of a bed.

Also be inventive when shopping at your local home center. Create a memorable bedroom light from an exterior fixture intended for porches and patios. Turn molding into a canopy that, coupled with coordinated fabric, can dress up an inexpensive bed.

This teen's room proves that clever design need not cost a fortune. Creative use of color and materials helps allow for personal expression.

Opposite: A chalkboard closet door is a handy spot to make to-do lists or jot down friends' phone numbers. Prime the doors first, then cover with chalkboard paint, which is available in aerosol spray and quart liquid at paint stores. After applying several coats let dry for three days before using.

Right: Old desks can be found for bargain prices at garage sales and thrift shops. If the top is unattractive or too rough to write on, cover it with a world map topped with a sheet of glass.

Bottom right: Conquer surface clutter with lots of storage options. A custom corkboard, framed by home center molding, can be made to fit any space. Hold magazines in flea market tin buckets. Divide open bookcases with wire and wicker baskets, which are perfect for CDs, video games, and books.

FOR INSTRUCTIONS ON MAKING TIN NOVELTY BASKETS, SEE PAGE 137.

FOR INSTRUCTIONS ON MAKING HOMEMADE CORKBOARD, SEE PAGE 137.

Your teen's room may never pass a white-glove test, but you can encourage him to tidy up by providing plenty of baskets, boxes, and bins to stash junk out of view.

system is installed directly on the wall, and the design continues through the bed platform and movable nightstands.

Like the shelves the custom corner desk is made of melamine and covered in plastic laminate. Extremely durable, laminate is available in many great patterns. Best of all, the crisp look is a snap to clean and maintain.

Accessories get the spotlight in this dugout. Create a personal Hall of Fame with memorabilia from your child's favorite teams or players. Real sports equipment, such as baseball bats and basketballs, meshes perfectly with the room's style and functions as usable art.

Opposite: Authentic details bring a theme to life. Genuine sports gear legitimizes this room's look. A supercool wall system doubles as an oversize headboard. The shelf unit, bracketed directly to the wall, sits on a separate base unit and integrates seamlessly with the bed.

Play Ball

Let your boy's passion for athletics fuel his room's decorating scheme. A sports theme will roll with his transformation from giggly tot to young man. Fill the room with all his favorite memorabilia and be sure to provide a prominent place to display them.

In this sleek, modern room, a floor-to-ceiling cabinet system occupies nearly a full wall and is illuminated by smart, cable-hung halogen lighting. The dimpled edges on the vertical boards add a funky touch. The wavy horizontal shelves are each carefully shaped from a piece of aluminum and attached to the vertical supports with screws. The entire

WORKING WITH A PRO

Installing an entire wall of built-in shelves or creating a custom desk is often best left to a professional carpenter or cabinetmaker. Finding a trustworthy pro is easy when you follow a few simple steps:
• Interview several candidates. Ask how long they have been in business, if they are licensed with the state, how many similar projects they completed in the last year, and what type of insurance they carry.
• Check references. Ask to see photos of at least three previous jobs. You also may want to visit former clients' homes to see the work firsthand.
• Get several bids. Provide the contractor with an exact description and your sketches of the job to get the most accurate estimate. Choose the person you feel most comfortable with, not necessarily the lowest bid.
• Sign a contract. It should spell out the who, what, where, when, and cost of your project. The more details you have in writing, the less likely a problem will arise later.
• Pay only when satisfied. Make the final payment when the work meets your standards and you are certain any subcontractors and suppliers have been paid.

Built-in furniture saves space in a
regulation-size bedroom.

Heavy Metal

Teens demand privacy—a luxury made more difficult if two are sharing a room. This big rectangular bedroom becomes a dream suite for a pair of boys thanks to a handy partition that divides the room into two distinct spaces.

The area behind the divider, which is farthest from the door, is the sleeping quarters. Jewel-tone bedding in gold, green, red, and amethyst allows each occupant to express individuality with personal color selections. Giant drawings of utensils and tools hang in pairs.

In front of the divider is a sitting area where the boys can hang out with friends.

Bold wire mesh chairs stand out against the inlay of inexpensive black automobile carpeting. The drum table is made from sheet metal wrapped around two plywood disks and topped with lava rocks.

The entire room benefits from vibrant walls drenched in midnight blue and deep orange. On the floor hard-wearing berber carpet in cream adds texture and light. Overhead light fixtures, made from conduit and shop lights, brighten both sides of the room. A 5-inch-deep galvanized metal channel runs the length of one wall, creating a massive display shelf that ties the two spaces together.

Above: Bold colors turn up visual heat in this shared space. Bright chenille bedspreads spice up the antique iron beds and provide textural contrast to the partition's steel-and-plastic surface.

Opposite: Light flows through the partition, which is made of inexpensive home center materials. Crafted of 2×4s, sheet metal, and roofing plastic, the industrial divider sets a contemporary tone for the rest of the room.

Metal panels are a fun background for magnetic words.

Simple Storage

A teenager comes with a lot of baggage. As a child grows he accumulates more clothes, books, sports equipment, and electronics. Finding storage space for all that stuff is just as important as choosing paint or bedding.

Keep things looking neat and orderly by making use of every square inch of the room. Use lots of clear bins, which allow a quick peek at the contents. Place smaller items in coordinated baskets on open shelves.

Make use of out-of-sight storage opportunities, including under the bed and in the closet. Invest in a closet storage system that uses drawers, shelves, and hanging space to maximize the small area. Buy a bed with built-in drawers or create a similar look by adding rolling boxes under a regular bed.

Below: Building a bed into an alcove opens the floors for a desk or seating area. Use the wall as a headboard by hanging glass shelves, which are a pretty way to keep special mementos out in the open.

Opposite: Mount a corkboard and hutch above a desk to double its storage capacity. Purchase an unfinished piece or look for a unit at a thrift store; give it new life with a coat of bright paint.

Decide how the room will be used and divide it accordingly. Spaces for sleep, play, and homework should be delineated by furniture layout.

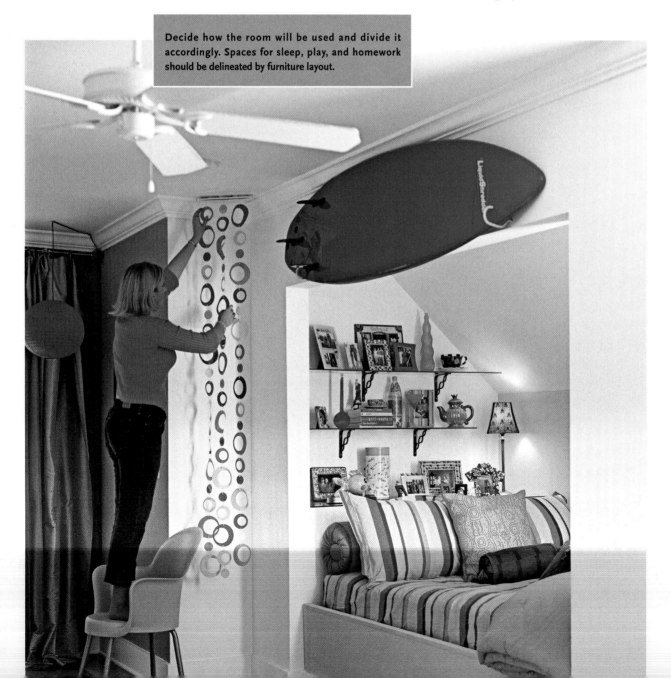

Other Spaces

Little Girl's Room

You have given your girl a bedroom she loves, but why stop there? Brighten her bathroom's disposition with these lively ideas. If you're running low on time and energy to decorate, don't worry. These one-hour wonders will transform the space without breaking your back or bank.

For a punch of style, pick two colors and use them in solid and patterned fabrics to create make-it-today decor. In this bathroom yellow walls are complemented by a strong accent color of watermelon. A polka-dot theme gives the space a bubbly personality, and the lighthearted projects provide extra zip.

Create a two-tone shower curtain by sewing two bath sheets together lengthwise and adding 13 grommets across the top. Cut various-size circles from coordinating washcloths and adhere them to the curtain with fabric glue. Add painted dots to accessories, such as the soap dish, using glass or porcelain paint, available at a crafts store. (These paints guarantee the dots won't wash away.)

Above right: Painted dots freckle a small ceramic bowl, which is perfect for storing jewelry or bath beads.

Right: Transform a basic frame into a memorable mirror. Paint a flat-front frame salmon pink; let dry. Using heavy-duty epoxy, glue a 2-inch-square tile in each corner of the frame. Glue two rows of 3/4-inch-square tiles between the corner pieces. On the tiles paint dots on alternating squares using glass or porcelain paints.

Opposite: In even the plainest room, a little creativity can wash on the style. Start with the bathroom basics—namely a sink, tub, and toilet—and add a playful dot motif for a bright and lively room sure to please a girl of any age.

In one hour or less, you can add amazing personality to your girl's bathroom.

FOR INSTRUCTIONS ON
MAKING THE BATH MATS,
SEE PAGE 138.

Flying Fun

Eliminate the bathtime blues by giving your son a bathroom that will spark his imagination. Choose a vivid color palette and a high-flying theme. This bathroom is ready for a dogfight, with sky-high walls and fabrics featuring dogs flying in propeller planes.

Coat the walls and ceiling in sky blue paint. Top-to-bottom use of the same color will make a cramped bathroom seem larger. Use a sponging technique to add white clouds. Give the floor a bird's-eye view by painting a grass green center and a blue border edged with white clouds.

In keeping with the up-in-the-air motif, glue cloudlike curves made of spongy molded rubber—found at a local home center—to the frame of an oversize mirror, chosen to make the room appear larger. Hang an upholstered valance that is fashioned to look like a large propeller.

Complete the theme by adding propeller hardware to the cabinets and airplains suspended from the ceiling.

Above: Use curtain fabric to make tab-top pockets to store toiletries and bath toys. Hang pockets from thick PVC pipes around the tub. Outfit the pipes with free-spinning propellers at both ends.

Opposite: Turning a simple white bathroom into an aviation adventure takes just a little paint, a few yards of fabric, and some inexpensive accessories.

Bathrooms are small and require no furnishing so redecorating them is quick, easy, and inexpensive.

BATHROOM SAFETY

Prevent accidents by always keeping a watchful eye when a child is in the bathroom. Also, follow these expert tips for keeping kids safe:

- Give kids a sturdy, tilt-proof step stool so they can safely reach the sink.
- Avoid falls with a slip-resistant bath mat on the floor and a rubber mat in the bathtub.
- Test the bathwater before the child gets in to prevent scalding. Also be sure the maximum temperature on your hot-water tank is no higher than 130 degrees.
- Install outlet covers and cabinet latches to keep children away from off-limits items.
- Keep medications and electrical appliances in childproof cabinets.
- Provide a low drawer or shelf for kids to store their toiletries and toys.

All-Weather Playroom

When the weather outside is frightful, make the kids' playroom a delightful alternative. This rainy-day retreat has fun places for kids to play and storage spots that Mom will appreciate.

Start with earth- and sky-inspired walls, ceiling, and floor. Paint the walls a springy blue. Create a sky above by painting the ceiling a slightly darker shade of blue and adding clouds. Complete the outdoor feeling with an artificial grass remnant underfoot. Purchase a piece of the easy-to-clean flooring at a home or garden store. Embellish the grass by stitching on several silk flowers and adding yellow rickrack on the edges with hotmelt adhesive.

Conceal messes with a chest and armoire. Provide easy access to supplies and toys with clear storage bins, a classic red wagon, and on-the-wall rain boots. Display a rotating selection of children's

artwork by using scallop frames with built-in pockets that allow you to easily slide new works in and out.

Finish the room with weather-theme accessories. Cover a plain white lampshade with a doll-size raincoat, add splashes of color with a rainbow lamp and bright fabrics, and display wooden letters that spell "rain" and "shine." Slickers, umbrellas, and boots act as decorative accents and dress-up clothes.

Right: A kid-size table with chairs or stools is an essential grouping for any play space. To complement the outdoor theme, choose a grassy green set and outfit the stools with fabric flower-petal covers.

Below: Upholstered armchairs are cozy spots for parent and child to read or watch a movie together. Hide unsightly items on a bookshelf behind a curtain hung from a tension rod.

Create cloud shapes on the ceiling using a brush and white interior latex paint. Adding a touch of blue to the paint makes the clouds look fluffier.

FOR INSTRUCTIONS ON MAKING FLOWER-PETAL STOOL COVERS, SEE PAGE 138.

Home School Cool

Transform an ordinary playroom into a fun learning den with a schoolhouse theme. Create a classic look with school surplus desks and chairs. Paint them

bright colors to freshen them up and add punch to the room, or purchase new vintage-look furniture on the Internet or from catalogs.

Make the room an interactive adventure with fun, educational activities. Create a chalkboard paint border that gives kids permission to draw on the walls. A molding ledge provides a spot to store erasers and chalk. Using magnet-backed letters children can play word games on a "learning tree" added to the wall with magnetic paint. A go-anywhere hopscotch rug allows for play, rain or shine.

Add meaningful touches with personalized canvas bins that can hide loads of toys. Let the kids have fun dressing up their notebooks with scrapbook supplies. Provide a spot for displaying friends' photos with pushpins or magnets on a busy bus message center.

Promote school spirit with a class-pride banner soaring in place of a window valance, along a wall as funky art, or stitched to a pillowcase. Felt pennants that highlight a child's graduation year get extra style with fun fringe and letterman-jacket-style numbers.

Opposite: Bring home a schoolhouse theme with a class banner, a flag, and snappy storage lockers. Soften the look by giving kids comfy chairs to flop into. Kids love curl-up spaces, so let them move smaller furniture around to suit their fancies.

Left: As children grow so do their homework requirements. Give them a special space to study (or do arts and crafts projects) by creating a comfortable desk area in one corner of the playroom.

Above: Inexpensive metal lunch boxes are smart spots to store toys and school supplies. Turn the boxes into fun message boards by adding homemade magnets. Simply glue letters cut from magazines to magnetic strips.

FOR INSTRUCTIONS ON MAKING A HOPSCOTCH RUG, SCHOOL BUS MESSAGE BOARD, AND PENNANT VALANCE, SEE PAGES 139-141.

Playtime can be educational when you supply interactive games and a cozy spot to read.

Creative Corner

When you have children you often have lots of stuff. Schoolwork, art, and crafts end up strewn about the house in a disorganized mess. Take control with a sleek studio that features parent-and-child workstations, a computer lab, and loads of storage space.

In this home a 10×13-foot formal dining room was transformed into a family office. If you don't have an entire room to turn over to artistic endeavors, use a corner of the family room or a portion of the basement. Make the most of a small space by maximizing the perimeter. Line the walls with desks and cabinets, leaving open floor space in the center for play.

Fill the space with existing furniture or make your own using simple, off-the-shelf materials from a home improvement center. These desks are hollow-core interior doors brushed with a marine-grade sealer for durability and finished with tapered metal legs purchased from a catalog. The shelving units are made with ¾-inch medium density fiberboard and screws.

The open shelves and desks are attached to the walls for stability, but everything else is on wheels for mobility. Underdesk caddies can be rolled out when needed and then tucked away neatly when not in use—no messy piles of papers in this space.

Opposite: Whether housed in a dedicated room or carved out of a basement corner, a sleek studio space is the perfect place for families to work and play together.

Right: Place portable art boxes on desktops to hold young artists' favorite supplies.

Below: Outfit a child's playroom or study space with plenty of storage units. This comprehensive cabinet features flat file drawers, vertical storage slots with adjustable dividers, and several storage bins that glide on rollers.

When everything has a place, supplies can be located quickly.

Store More

Converting a bonus room or basement into a spacious playroom is a great option. It gives kids room to spread out while keeping their mess hidden behind closed doors. If space is at a premium in your home, however, devoting an entire room to child's play may be difficult.

Instead try this space-saving idea Invest in a generic piece of furniture, such as a TV or computer armoire, and customize it to suit your child's needs. An upright playroom maximizes vertical space while serving as Command Central for toys, games, art supplies, dress-up clothes, and more.

If purchasing a new armoire is out of the budget, check garage sales for a gently used piece or search the Internet for an unfinished, ready-to-assemble option and give it new life with a few coats of primer and paint.

Consider painting the unit basic white or black and filling it with portable storage in kid-friendly colors. A neutral-color armoire can evolve as your child's tastes change or can be used later in another room of the house.

Opposite: An armoire door coated with chalkboard paint serves double duty. Cover the panel areas of the door or, if your door is flat, simply mark off borders with painter's tape before painting.

Below: A see-through bin gives a child a sneak peek at its contents, preventing the grab-and-throw approach to searching for a toy. Take stock of toys before buying storage containers so you can choose bins in appropriate sizes.

Right: Use built-in drawers to hold large items, such as trucks and stuffed animals. Label each drawer with letter stencils or, for kids who are too young to read, paint pictures of the items that go inside (use paint pens for detail).

QUICK CHANGE

Transform a computer armoire into a child's play station with these five simple ideas:
1. Hot-glue painted corkboard to the inside back and inside door to create a gallery for your child's artwork. Painting the cork the same color as the walls gives the piece a coordinated look.
2. Encourage more artwork with easy-to-reach roller paper. Install eye hooks beneath the top shelf; hold paper on a dowel cut about 4 inches longer than the roll.
3. Make good use of built-in accessories: Label drawers for toys, turn an inside door into a chalkboard, and use the keyboard slider for storing canvases or puzzles in progress.
4. Provide plenty of plastic containers for storing art supplies and smaller toys.
5. Reserve the top shelf for games and toys that are used less often; make the bottom bins home to daily favorites.

How To

Ideas & Projects

Inspired by rooms or ideas seen in this book? Get the look and add a personal touch to your child's room with the simple decorating projects in this chapter.

Above: Fabric-covered art (project shown on page 25)

Supplies
- Coordinating fabrics
- Fabric scissors
- Needle and thread
- Artist's canvas frames
- Heavy-duty stapler and staples

1. Cut coordinating fabrics in desired shapes. Coloring books can provide inspiration for simple shapes.

2. Hand-appliqué the shapes to a square or rectangular piece of fabric until your masterpiece is complete.

3. Stretch the artwork over frames used for artist's canvas and staple the fabric to the back of the frame.

Below: Painted wall technique (project shown on page 26)

Supplies
- Green base-coat paint
- Blue paint for scallops
- Paintbrush
- Scallop stencil
- Thick plastic for stencil (optional)

1. Apply a base coat of green paint to the entire wall.

2. At shoulder height stencil blue scallops to mimic the look of a wave. Contiue the blue paint to the ceiling. If desired, paint the ceiling blue for added dimension.

3. Freehand paint polka dots. To make the dots more uniform, make a stencil by tracing a juice glass rim onto thick plastic and cutting it out. Position the stencil randomly on the wall and paint.

• Hot-glue gun and hot-glue adhesive
• Ribbon, trims, and buttons
1. Trace the lid, lid sides, and sides of a cardboard hatbox onto fabric and cut out, adding a little extra to each edge.
2. Use spray adhesive to adhere fabric pieces to the box. Wrap extra fabric underneath and inside box; for the lid adhere fabric to the top first, then to the sides.
3. Hot glue ribbon, trims, and buttons to the lid for flourish.

Below: Hanger hooks (project shown on page 29)
Supplies
• Wood hangers
• Saw
• Paint or stain (optional)
• Wood board
• Screwdriver and screws
1. Cut wood hangers about an inch or two away from the hook.
2. Paint or stain a wood board to match the room's decor.
3. Position the hangers upside down on the board and attach with screws.

Above: Affordable framed art (from room shown on page 27)
Supplies
• Wood frames with plain white mats
• Pink paint
• Paintbrush
• Scrapbook paper
• Scissors
• Rubber cement
1. Coat the frames with pink paint; let dry.
2. To make the colorful mats, cut scrapbook paper $\frac{1}{2}$ inch smaller all around than the original opening, with an interior opening $\frac{1}{2}$ inch larger all around than the original.
3. Secure the new pink mat to the original white one with rubber cement.

Above right: Hatbox storage (project shown on page 27)
Supplies
• Hatbox
• Pencil or chalk
• Fabric
• Scissors
• Spray adhesive

Below: Nautical tieback (Project shown on page 36)

Supplies
• Baltic birch plywood
• Sailboat stencil
• Pencil
• Jigsaw
• Acrylic paints and paintbrushes
• Wood dowel
• Screwdriver and double-ended screws

1. Use a sailboat stencil to draw a boat shape onto an 8-inch-square piece of Baltic birch plywood.

2. Cut the shape out using a jigsaw.

3. Paint the boat with acrylic paints. Not an artist? Paint the shape a solid color for a bold, graphic look.

4. Attach the holdback to a 3-inch-long dowel with wood glue.

5. Attach the holdback to the wall with double-ended screws.

Above: Nautical window treatment (Project shown on page 36)

Supplies
• Blue and white ticking fabric
• Fabric scissors
• Measuring tape or yardstick
• Nylon roping
• Large grommets
• Wood dowel
• Red spray paint

1. Cut fabric about $1\frac{1}{2}$ times the window width to create gentle, wavelike folds when the valance is hung.

2. Add large grommets, spaced about 8 inches apart, along the top of the fabric.

3. Paint the dowel red and mount it above the window.

4. Weave nylon roping, available from home centers, through the grommets and around the dowel rod.

Below: Fabric-covered knobs (Project shown on page 41)

Supplies
- Fabric
- Fabric scissors
- Crafts glue
- Decoupage medium
- Paintbrush

1. Cut a fabric square twice as wide as the knob.

2. Apply crafts glue to the back of the fabric square; cover the knob with the fabric.

3. Cut slits around the edges and fold the fabric flat on the knob's backside; cut off excess fabric.

4. Cover the fabric with decoupage medium to give it a protective coating.

Above: Shadow-box art (Project shown on page 39)

Supplies
- Shadow-box frame
- Fabric or scrapbook paper
- Spray adhesive
- Punch-out paper dolls
- Scissors
- Double-sided foam tape

1. Cover the background mat that comes with the frame with fabric or scrapbook paper using spray adhesive.

2. Punch out several paper dolls and place a tiny square of double-sided foam tape on the back of each one. Press the dolls onto the covered mat and return the mat to the frame.

Above: Picket-fence bed (Project shown on page 46)

Supplies
- Bed frame
- 2×4 boards cut the width of the bed frame
- Pickets (eight were used on each end of the bed in this example; the number needed will vary with the bed size, picket size, and spacing)
- Four porch posts or newels
- Four finials to top the posts
- Tape measure
- Saw
- Sandpaper
- Tack cloth
- Latex paint
- Paintbrush
- Clean rags
- Wood glue
- Hammer
- Nails
- Wood filler
- Screws for attaching the frame to the headboard and footboard (size varies with the openings on the frame)
- Washers (optional)

1. Measure the ends of the bed frame. The newels or porch posts should fit at the outer corners of the frame. Use this measurement to determine the length of three pieces of 2×4 lumber that form the structure at the head of the bed and the two pieces of 2×4 that will create the foot of the bed.

2. Calculate the desired height of the newels (with finials) and the pickets. This will vary depending on your taste, the height of the frame, and the depth of the mattress. Note that on the headboard shown, the pickets are tallest in the center and decrease in height toward each end.

3. Cut the boards to size. Note: A home improvement center can do this for you at a minimal charge. Be sure to have your measurements with you and mark the order and placement for each piece as it is cut.

4. Sand the pieces until smooth. Wipe them clean with a tack cloth.

5. Paint each piece with at least two coats of latex paint. Note: For a whitewashed look, try using paint that has been diluted to the consistency of cream, then use a rag to wipe off some of the excess before the paint dries. For a rustic, aged look, use a crackle medium.

6. Glue and nail the posts to the ends of the three 2×4s at the head of the bed and the two 2×4s at the foot of the bed. The ends of the 2×4s should align with the outer edges of the posts.

7. Turn the above pieces so the 2×4s lie against the floor. Glue and nail the pickets into place, spacing them evenly. Fill the nail holes with wood filler and touch up with paint.

8. Turn the headboard and footboard upright.

9. Attach the headboard and footboard to the bed frame with screws. (Openings in the frame should allow for this; if the screw head is too small and slips through the hole, place a washer between the frame and the screw head.)

10. Glue the finials into place.

Supplies
- Tape measure
- Self-adhesive shelf paper
- Scissors
- Latex paint
- Glaze
- 3-inch paintbrush
- Flat wallpaper sponge
- Acetate
- Painter's tape
- Sea sponge
- 1-inch flat artist's brushes

1. Starting with white walls, use self-adhesive shelf paper to create a mask for the white spaces on which the flowers will be painted. Measure the walls to determine what size frame fits the scale of your room. (This room used 10×14-inch rectangles.) Cut enough rectangles for the number of motifs desired. Working on one wall at a time, determine the placement of the flowers and adhere each rectangle.

2. Mix one part latex paint with three parts glaze. Using a 3-inch brush and working in about a 2-foot-square space, load the brush with paint and apply with circular strokes until the brush is dry. Then dip a flat wallpaper sponge into plain glaze and dab glaze over the brushstrokes to soften the effect. Use about the same amount of paint on your brush each time to achieve a consistent finish. As you complete a wall and while the glaze is still wet, carefully remove the shelf paper.

3. Cut simple bloom shapes from acetate to create stencils. Make a leaf stencil to accompany each flower. (The stem will be painted freehand.) When the walls are dry, tape the bloom and leaf stencils to the wall to form a flower within the white rectangle. Dip a sea sponge into the desired-color paint, then into clear glaze,

and blend the mixture by lightly tapping the sponge on paper. Dab at the wall to fill in the stencil shape.

4. Remove the stencils and paint a freehand line for the flower stem using a 1-inch flat artist's brush and a paint-glaze mixture. After the flower dries use a 1-inch brush and another paint-glaze mixture to add a border to the rectangle.

fabric with a hot-glue gun and stick the corresponding side of the tape to the arched PVC.

4. For the peaked cabana "roof," push the top panel down through a towel ring attached to the wall at the desired height. Remove or secure extra fabric that falls into the cabana. Let the roof panel extend about 6 inches over the wall panels and trim it with fabric and ball fringe.

5. A final tip: Use drapery weights on the overlapping ruffle and on the bottom of the panels to help the cabana hang better.

Above and right: Cool cabana (project shown on page 59)

Supplies

• Three lengths of polyvinyl chloride (PVC) piping (it should reach almost to the ceiling)

• Four T-shape plastic plumbing brackets

• Four plastic plumbing couplings

• Four fabric shower curtains

• Hook-and-loop tape

• Hot-glue gun and hot-glue adhesive

• Plastic towel ring

• Drapery weights

1. Choose a section of wall that is at least 4 feet wide (windowless corners work well too). Adjust the height and width to suit the child's age and the ceiling height.

2. For the cabana frame, stand two PVC lengths on the floor and attach them to the floor with couplings. Bend the third PVC length into an arc and attach the two vertical pieces to the arched PVC with T-shape brackets, as shown above. Attach to the wall at the height of the cabana "walls" with the other two couplings.

3. For the fabric cover use one shower curtain for each side panel and two sewn together lengthwise for the top. To make the cabana "walls," use hook-and-loop tape: Attach one side of the tape to the

Above left: Window shade (project shown on page 60)

Supplies
- Fabric
- Fabric scissors
- Measuring tape or yardstick
- Sewing machine and thread
- Iron
- 1×2-inch piece of wood
- Saw
- Heavy-duty stapler and staples
- Screwdriver and screws

1. Cut two fabric pieces to fit inside a window frame, plus seam allowances on all sides and an extra 2 inches at the top.
2. Sew with wrong sides together, leaving an opening. Turn, sew opening shut, and press. Topstitch ties to top.
3. Cut a 1×2-inch piece of wood to the width of the fabric and staple to the top backside.
4. To hang, screw through the wood and into the top window frame.

Above right: Cabana-style cornice (project shown on page 93)

Supplies
- Purchased plywood cornice
- Hammer
- Small brads or cup hooks
- Nails or screwdriver and screws
- Floral string lights
- Dried palm leaves

- Heavy-duty stapler and staples
- Protective gloves

1. Nail small brads or screw in cup hooks about a foot apart in a row on the underside of the plywood cornice to hold the cord of the floral string lights. Hang the cornice using a hammer and nails or screwdriver and screws.
2. Drape the flower lights on the front side of the cornice and arrange and staple dried palm leaves around the lights. Wear protective gloves, or the palm leaves will cause cuts. The leaves should not be in direct contact with the lightbulbs.

Below right: Graphic artwork (project shown on page 94)

Supplies
- Old textbooks, colorful tissue paper
- Scissors
- Artist's canvas
- Glue
- Wide paintbrush

1. Find text with words or phrases that speak to you. You also can print words from your computer. Use a copy machine to enlarge the text, making extras and enlarging some portions more than others. Trim closely around the text.
2. Cut color tissue paper into simple shapes with irregular edges. Try tearing the tissue paper for a more random effect.
3. Experiment by moving the words and

tissue paper around on a piece of artist's canvas until you like the composition. Avoid positioning a key element in the center of the canvas—a perfectly centered item visually chops the image in half.
4. Dilute glue with water (about 3 parts glue to 1 part water). Use a wide paintbrush to brush glue over the artist's canvas, then adhere the text. Brush on another coat of the glue solution to seal.
5. While the glue is still wet, apply the tissue paper. When the tissue paper gets wet from the glue, it becomes translucent and words pasted underneath will be visible.

This page: Molding canopy (Project shown on page 104)

Supplies
- Desired molding ($2\frac{1}{2}$-inch dentil molding was used for the project shown)
- Measuring tape
- Saw
- Stud finder
- Pencil
- $1\frac{1}{2}$- or 2-inch finishing nails (for nailer)
- Pneumatic nailer
- Construction or hotmelt adhesive (optional)
- Wood putty
- Caulk
- Sandpaper
- Tack cloth
- Latex paint and paintbrush
- Fabric (yardage depends on height of ceiling and number of panels)
- Needle and thread
- Heavy-duty stapler and staples

1. Determine the placement of molding on the ceiling. Ideally one length should be under a joist. Measure to determine the lengths of the molding, cut the pieces, and miter the ends that will meet. (Crosscut the ends that will abut the wall.)

2. Locate joists with a stud finder; mark locations with a pencil.

3. Use a pneumatic nailer and $1\frac{1}{2}$- or 2-inch finishing nails to secure molding to the ceiling, spacing nails so they go into the joists. (You also can use construction or hotmelt adhesive to attach the molding; however, this can tear the drywall's paper face when you remove the molding.)

4. Fill holes with putty and apply caulk between molding and the ceiling; let dry.

5. Sand, wipe with tack cloth, and paint; let dry.

6. Cut panels to desired length plus $\frac{1}{2}$ inch for bottom hem and 2 inches for attaching to molding. Hem bottoms. Gather panels; staple tops to the back of the molding.

Above: Tin novelty baskets (project shown on page 105)

Supplies
- Tin bucket or basket
- Sandpaper
- Latex primer
- Latex paint
- Paintbrushes
- Candle
- Drop cloth or newspapers
- Stud finder
- Hammer and nail

1. To paint, first lightly sand, clean, and prime the bucket with latex primer recommended for metal. Allow to dry. Paint with a latex base coat.

2. To simulate aging rub a candle over the dry bucket. Concentrate on the corners and the edges.

3. Paint a top coat with latex paint. Choose paint in complementary color combinations. Allow to dry.

4. Place a drop cloth or newspapers under the bucket to catch sanded dust. Sand with a medium-grade sandpaper, allowing the top coat to sand off wherever the wax was applied, exposing the base coat. Sand with a smooth, light motion.

5. To hang, locate a stud and nail securely into the wall.

Below: Homemade corkboard (project shown on page 105)

Supplies
- Tape measure
- Pencil
- One 4×8-foot sheet of $\frac{1}{4}$-inch plywood
- Circular or tablesaw
- Roll of cork (available at crafts supply stores and home centers)
- Scissors
- Crafts glue or rubber cement
- 1-inch drywall screws
- Stud finder
- Electric drill with screwdriver tip
- Molding (enough for the perimeter of the bulletin board)
- Corner rosettes (optional)
- 4d finishing nails
- Wood putty
- Sandpaper
- Tack cloth
- Paint or stain

1. Use a tape measure to determine the size of the bulletin board, allowing for the molding border. Pencil its placement on the wall.

2. Use a circular or tablesaw to cut plywood to the size of the bulletin board; use scissors to cut a panel of cork to the same size as the plywood.

3. Attach the cork to the plywood with crafts glue or rubber cement.

4. Fasten the plywood and the cork to the wall studs using an electric drill with a screwdriver tip and 1-inch drywall screws.

5. Use a circular or tablesaw to cut the molding to length to border the bulletin board, mitering the ends if desired. Alternatively, use corner rosettes to join the horizontal and vertical pieces of molding.

6. Fasten molding to the wall with 4d finishing nails.

7. Fill holes with putty, let dry, then sand smooth. Wipe with a tack cloth.

8. Paint or stain as desired.

Below: Polka-dot bath mats (project shown on page 115)

Supplies
- Paper
- Fabric scissors
- Two bath mats in contrasting colors
- Heavy-duty needle and thread

1. Cut paper circles to use as templates.
2. Trace the circles on the back of each mat, marking the same number of circles in the same sizes on each mat (so each one, for example, has one large, three small, and two medium circles).
3. Cut out circles from mats, using good-quality fabric scissors to cut right on the circle line; don't start cutting from the edge of the mat. Remove the cut circles.
4. Reposition circles in the contrasting mat.
5. Working on the wrong side of the mats, hand-sew each circle along the raw edge.

Above: Flower-petal stool covers (project shown on page 119)

Supplies
- Child-size stool
- Yellow quilting fabric
- Fabric scissors
- Button
- Needle and thread
- Sewing machine
- Fiberfill
- Red felt

1. Cut two circles slightly larger than the tops of the stools from quilting fabric and attach a button to the center of each one. for a tufted top.
2. Place the two right sides facing each other and machine-sew the edge, leaving enough room to stuff.
3. Turn right side out, stuff, and sew shut.
4. For the petals cut shapes from sheets of red felt—five or six per cushion, depending on the size of the petal—then hand-stitch or machine-sew the petals to the edge of the cushion.

Above: Hopscotch rug (shown on page 120)

Supplies
- Ruler, pencil
- Card stock or cardboard
- Scissors
- 36×60-inch sisal rug with a rubber backing
- Red permanent marking pen
- 8-inch-tall number stencils
- Paintbrush
- Red acrylic paint
- Fabric glue
- 7 yards of red double-fold bias tape
- 5½ yards of 1½-inch-wide red-and-white checked ribbon
- 5½ yards of 1¼-inch-wide red rickrack

1. Draw a 10×11½-inch rectangle on card stock; cut out for a pattern. Fold the rectangle in half to mark the center on the long sides, then open the rectangle. Find the center on one short end of the rug (this will be the bottom edge).

2. Center the rectangle 3½ inches from the center bottom of the rug. With the permanent marking pen, trace the shape.

3. Add the rest of the rectangles to the rug, referring to the photo, above, for placement.

4. Place a number stencil in the center of each rectangle; outline the number with the marking pen. Remove the stencil, then paint the number with red acrylic paint. Repeat for all numbers.

5. Cut and glue pieces of bias tape around the rectangles to cover the lines you drew.

6. Glue the checked ribbon on the top of the rug along all four edges. Add rickrack to the backside, letting half of the rickrack peek around the edge.

7. Finish with a skid-proof rubber backing to hold steady for lots of hopping.

Supplies
- Tracing paper, pencil, ruler, scissors
- Water-soluble marking pen, fabric glue
- 10×18-inch rectangles of felt in your child's school colors
- 1-yard lengths of assorted trims: pompom fringe, rickrack, and 1½-inch-wide ruffled ecru cotton
- 1-inch-wide ribbon for pennant hanging loops: red and white checked (1 foot for each pennant)
- Adhesive-backed embroidered letter and number appliqués
- ¼-inch-diameter decorative cording, cut to the width of your window plus 12 inches
- Decorative window rod, finials, and hardware for hanging

1. Draw a long, skinny triangle on plain kraft paper to use as a pattern.

2. Using the water-soluble marking pen, trace around the patterns on felt, making one long triangle and one border strip for each pennant. Cut out the shapes from contrasting felt colors.

3. Place a contrasting border strip along the short edge of each triangle. Glue the pieces together, letting the border strip overlap the triangle ¼ inch.

4. Glue the edge of one 1-yard trim to the wrong side of one triangle, placing the trim along the two long edges. Repeat for all the triangles.

5. Cut the ribbon into two 6-inch lengths for each pennant. Fold each ribbon in half and glue the cut ends together, then glue the cut ends to the wrong side of the pennant on the border strip.

6. Position and press embroidered letters and numbers to the front of each pennant.

7. String the pennants on the decorative cording. Tie the ends to the window rod's finials for a valance.

Above: School bus message board (project shown on page 121)

Supplies
- Tracing paper, pencil, ruler, scissors
- 13×36-inch sheet of thin cork
- Paintbrushes
- Acrylic paints: yellow, black, white, light blue, and silver
- Black permanent marking pen
- Six 3¾-inch-square cork coasters for windows
- Two 4-inch-diameter cork coasters for wheels
- Thick white crafts glue
- Adhesive magnetic tape
- 1-inch-tall black letter stickers
- 2½-inch square of red adhesive-backed felt
- ½-inch-tall white letter stickers
- Removable mounting stickers

1. Using the photo above as a guide to draw a bus shape onto tracing paper, then enlarge it on a photocopier to fit the cork; cut out the pattern. Trace the pattern onto the sheet of cork and cut out the shape.

2. Paint the bus yellow. Let the paint dry. With a pencil and ruler, draw details on the bus. Referring to the photo, above, paint the details using black and white paints and the black marking pen.

3. Paint square coasters light blue (windows) and round coasters black (wheels). Add a circle of silver paint to the center of each wheel; add details with marking pen. Glue windows and wheels to the bus.

4. Cut two 21-inch strips of magnetic tape. Press the strips to the bus in parallel rows spaced 2 inches apart. Spell "SCHOOL BUS" with black letter stickers, placing words between the magnetic strips.

5. Cut out an octagon shape from red felt. Spell "STOP" with the white letter stickers on the red felt sign. Press the stop sign in place.

6. Use mounting stickers to hold the bus to the wall.

Index

transform ordinary to
extraordinary